IT STARTED WITH A SIT

The book to help expectant and new parents of both kids and dogs.

Debby Lucken

To Tina,

happy reading!

Debby x

To my husband Gary and all our children, Pixel, Molly, Wilco, Winnie and Mario, with love.

Praises For The Book

"'It Started with Sit is akin to having casual afternoon tea and a chat with storyteller, Debby Lucken.

Written as a memoir, she reflects on her early connection and longing for a dog of her own, then takes her readers on her journey of getting married, and finally getting the dog of her dreams.

She shares their challenges of blending their cherished dog and new baby into a cohesive family using a 'that was then, this is now' writing style that will speak to expectant couples.

Lucken shares their initial inexperienced perspectives as new dog guardians and new parents, and then reflects on their experiences with her current seasoned knowledge of being a professional dog trainer and experienced mother.

Lucken has since created a well-received organization, Kids Around Dogs, that successfully educates families and professionals about creating safe, dynamic relationships between families and dogs.'

~ Melissa Y. Winkle, OTR/L, FAOTA,CPDT-KA

President, Dogwood Therapy Services

President, Animal Assisted Intervention International Instructor University of North Florida, AAI Certificate Program

'A delightful memoir filled with real life love, adventure and tips for successful living with a baby and a beloved dog. This memoir is one every dog lover will relate to, especially prior to having a baby. The experiences of Pixel and her Mom and Dad and then Molly are something we can all enjoy and learn from. I enjoyed reading this lovely book and look forward to the next one of the series.'

~ Jennifer Shryock B.A. CDBC
Founder/Director of Family Paws Parent Education

'This really is a joyful journey through one mother's life - from moving countries to raising kids & dogs together. "It started with a sit" weaves in wonderful tips for multi-species households amongst this biographical tale.
I thoroughly enjoyed getting to know Debby and her family better as they crossed many waters, growing incredible relationships together.

As a Mother myself, it was lovely to re-live Debby's journey through pregnancy and beyond - to hear of the regrets and lessons learned. Ultimately we know that relationships with our kids and our dogs will always be a magical one filled with love.

As a pet professional, I know this book with help many families as they consider embarking on a life of children and dogs living in harmony together.

~ Caroline Wilkinson,
Certified Animal Behaviourist and trainer, founder of Barket Place

'"It Started With A Sit" is the first book by KAD founder Debby Lucken.

The book takes you on a journey through Debby's own experiences of life as a dog loving child, through to the present day where she is both a mother and dog parent.

Debby teaches all the common sense approaches she has learned over the years, ensuring that the children and dogs of the family get along happily together. Safety is always paramount when it comes to children and dogs, and Debby considers every angle from pregnancy right through childhood, while fostering a friendly, loving relationship at every stage. A brilliant book for all parents and carers of young people, and I can't wait to see what Debby writes next!"

~ Freya V. Locke
Dog Behaviourist, Author, Blogger
Founder of 'Fun Not Fear® ' Club

Connect with me

I hope you enjoyed my book!
If would like to stay in touch with me and let me know how parenting kids and dogs is going for you, **follow me on social media**.

Facebook Group:
www.facebook.com/groups/KADkidsarounddogs

Facebook:
www.facebook.com/Kidsarounddogs

Instagram:
www.instagram.com/kadkidsarounddogs

X (formerly known as Twitter):
twitter.com/kidsarounddogs

YouTube Channel:
@kadkidsarounddogs

Website:
www.kidsarounddogs.co.uk

Contents

Introduction

People often say; 'Write about what you know'. This is why I will take you on a journey through my life experience around dogs and kids such as what inspired me to develop and launch Kids Around Dogs® and what it all means to me.

At times, life takes you on unique twists and turns, which are of particular importance and can have larger consequences when children are involved. Our children's development can have a powerful impact on our lives, in our dogs' lives and in the way we adapt to these inevitable changes.

As we watch our children develop, we understand, appreciate, welcome, and even expect some changes, especially the big ones, like them walking and talking. But what about our dogs? How can they understand and come to appreciate the arrival of a new person in the family? How can they learn how to accept the new events a baby brings to the household?

The first book in this series, 'It Started with a Sit', tells you the story of how I became the mother of a dog and a child. How we built our family from 'just' a couple, to welcoming a dog, and then a child; and how, as a family, we helped our dog to be happy around our newborn baby.

Although this is my journey, I feel that many people will be able to relate to what life as a mother of dogs and kids is for me, especially during the first stages of parenthood.

Together, we will walk through my story as a certified dog behaviourist, dog trainer, and founder of Kids Around Dogs®. I will also highlight important points to understand and ways that you can best arrange your life, your home and your environment for a life of babies and toddlers around dogs.

Chapter 1:

My Childhood Without a Dog

I was born in the south of Switzerland, a lovely city called Lugano, where people speak Italian, are typically rather posh and pooches are plenty.

Switzerland is a beautiful country, but also very expensive, so even back then, both my parents were working.

When I was very little, my father worked during the day, while my mother looked after my older brother, Davide, and me. Then my mother would work most evenings, while my dad would take care of us kids.

Later, when I was about 5, my parents moved to another town and got better jobs. This meant that my dad was then gone for most of the day, while my mum would work in the mornings, leaving the afternoons for chores and us kids.

A pet of any kind was out of discussion, let alone one that needed constant care, such as a dog.

Despite never having a dog in our home, that never stopped me from being completely fascinated by these wonderful creatures. My family often recalls how even when I was very little and was in the pushchair, I would go nuts if I saw dogs and didn't get to pet them.

My mother also recalls how I loved humans and was also keen on displaying affection towards strangers. She often tells me how I wanted to give kisses to random people!

Luckily, while keeping my love for both canine and human species, I now know better than wanting to stroke every dog I meet and wanting to hug or kiss strangers on the street.

Life is nothing, if not a lesson.

As I mentioned before, just before I turned 6 years old, we moved to a smaller town near Lugano. With my dad's better job, he was working longer hours and was often very stressed out and tired. My mother got a part-time job in the morning, while both Davide and I were at school. This balanced out well for everyone, and I remember hoping that once we were all settled, I could convince my family to get a dog.

However, even my brother was against the idea and so I was fighting a losing battle.

Just recently I found the diaries I kept while growing up. Across so many pages I refer to dogs and how wonderful it would have been to have one.

Also, the reality was that I struggled to make real friends and, although I was sociable and had many acquaintances, I always felt disconnected from my peers.

In my heart, I knew that the love of a dog would have made it all better. I was sure that having a canine companion would have made me feel part of something special and that he or she would have understood me like no other human seemed to be able to.

However, my family never budged... I was not allowed to have a dog and that was final.

But in 1993, when I turned 13, my mother got me a part-time job: dog walking! And I could not have been happier!

I only had one client; a chunky black Labrador named Theo.

His humans worked in the building our apartment was in, so I didn't need to worry about transportation to get back and forth to him. Moreover, the walking sessions – meant to be twice a day – were flexible, so I could choose when to go pick him up and when to return him. As the job was during the summer holidays.

I didn't have school to worry about, but I still had homework and the occasional outings with my mother. I don't recall meeting up with anyone from school over the holidays, but perhaps I did and simply forgot about it. To me, the summer of 1993 was all about Theo.

His humans, a lovely couple who absolutely adored their dog, had instructed me not to take him out if it was too hot; that he was great off the lead, loved playing with big rocks and was not that interested in tennis balls, so not to bother with those.

I remember how excited I was to go out on our first walk alone, as we had a couple of walks with his humans first, to get him used to me.

I went to their office in the morning, picked him up, and off we went on a walk nearby, where dogs were allowed off the lead, and there were rocks for him to play with.

Theo was a gorgeous Labrador, but he was not the leanest of dogs, and his guardians had failed to mention that he would struggle if walked too much, which I had no idea could happen to a dog. As a 13-year-old girl, I simply assumed all dogs loved to run and they could do it all day.

And so, on that first walk, I learned my first lesson about dogs: they also get tired and need to rest.

After leaving the office and letting Theo off the lead to have a run and a sniff, he started picking up rocks, really big ones! So, I threw them for him, a bit like you would with a ball. He seemed to love that game and would go find the rock and bring it back to me. I had a fantastic time with him! Then, after a few minutes, Theo lay down with the giant rock in his mouth and would not walk anymore.

I tried calling him, getting another rock, walk a few steps away... he simply would not move. I didn't know what to do! Bear in mind, we didn't have mobile phones back then, so I couldn't just call somebody to come help me. It was just me and Theo, and Theo wasn't listening, nor was he moving!

After attempting everything I could think of, I just stood by his side, as he rested laying down on the ground with his giant rock by the side of his long, beautiful mouth.

I couldn't do anything but indulge him and talk to him. I told him about how his mother would not want me back if she knew I couldn't handle it; I begged him to simply walk back with me to the office where he would be resting in his bed and with air conditioning on for hours before my next visit.

We stayed like that for a long time, and finally, after a while, he stood up and carried on walking. Slowly, and while still carrying his rock, we managed to make our way back to the office, and to his bed, water, and air conditioning.

About 4 hours after dropping him off, I went back to take him for our second walk of the day. However, when I showed up that afternoon, Theo was resting and wouldn't even lift his head when I approached him. I was told he hadn't moved from that position since I had returned him after our morning walk.

He wasn't used to walking much those days, as his guardians were both too busy with work.

I went over to Theo and tried to convince him to follow me, but he wouldn't have it. So, his guardians suggested I come back the following morning, as originally agreed, and try again.

Over the summer Theo and I bonded amazingly well! His stamina and body were greatly improved, and he was much leaner, fitter, and happier for it. And so was I.

When school started again in September, our walks had to stop, as I couldn't be around for Theo, however, I would see him occasionally and he would run to me with as much love and joy as ever. At the time, nothing, and I mean nothing, gave me as much happiness as those times.

Many years later, Theo passed away from cancer. When I was told, even though I hadn't seen him in a very long time, I cried. He was my friend, and I will never forget how happy and loved he made me feel. Now, this was over 30 years ago, but I still remember those feelings and the love I had and will always have for Theo. The power of dogs is incredible.

The dream of having a dog never left me, but I did eventually, in my late teens, stop asking my parents for one. I knew what their answer would be, and I then had other things to focus on.

One of my goals was going to study English as a foreign language in Oxford, England, which I started when I was 19. Only a few years later, at 22, I moved to London permanently. After a few months there, I met my now-husband, Gary, who is from North London.

Amongst his many qualities, he loves dogs! Although he might have been a bit more of a cat person when I first met him. Nothing wrong with that, of course, but I have always put dogs on a pedestal, and I knew the person I was to share my life with had to feel the same.

Gary and I got married when I was 26 and that summer we adopted Pixel, a beautiful and cheeky Pug, who stole our hearts entirely.

With all that love for dogs, and the strong desire to adopt a dog, I had to wait 26 long years to have my own. 26 long years during which my heart was never fully whole, 26 long years my clothes were never covered in dog fur and the responsibilities of caring for another living creature weren't part of my life.

Key Points

I feel that whether the topic is about becoming a parent of a human or a dog, the thing we can all agree on is that it comes with an incredible number of responsibilities.

On one hand, you need to make sure you help a baby become a polite and happy adult. You ought to keep this human safe and protected, while also ensuring he or she is independent enough to make their own life experiences and choices.

On the other hand, you have this amazing creature, who, although very different in appearance from humans; knows about our feelings, can read us better than we read ourselves, and has the power to hurt us more than we care to imagine.

That is why we need to be fully responsible for dogs too: we need to ensure to adopt them from reputable breeders or ethical rescue centres; we need to select the right breed for our lifestyle; we need to provide them with the right education, which follows positive and kind methods; and we need to learn about dogs! We need to know how they communicate with us; how their life is theirs to integrate into ours, but that they still have the freedom of safe choices and preferences and opinions.

In case it wasn't clear, I strongly believe a dog is part

of the family.

All my dogs are my children, but they are still animals, and we should allow them to be dogs. I am grateful to my parents for saying no to a dog for me.

I feel that too often parents adopt dogs because the children desperately want one. There will be tears and a million promises from the kids that they will look after the dog, and they will clean up after the puppy. They will do it all. And so, the parents, worn out by their relentless children, adopt a dog.

Don't get me wrong, I know a lot of parents who got a dog because of the kids but ended up loving the dog more than anything or anyone ever and sometimes they even prefer the dog to the kids and some days, I get that!

However, we ought to be considering multiple factors when adopting a dog, and one big one should be not to adopt a dog just because the kids want one. A dog is a living being, with ideas, emotions, needs, and wants. A dog isn't a toy that the child 'gets to have'.

We could send children the wrong messages about animals if we adopt a dog just because the child wants to. If a child asks for a dog the way he/she asks for a new videogame, and gets it, the dog 'loses' value in the heart and mind of the child, who might think the dog is something the kid gets to have as a thing, rather than a sentient being to respect, love and care for.

It is very important to make sure kids know that a dog isn't a commodity and teaching them the value of a living creature is crucial at any age.

Before you decide to get a dog, have a family meeting, and get everyone to write down 5 reasons they want a dog and 5 reasons why they should not get a dog. If your children are too little to write, make sure to help them out, or to let them draw what they want to say. It is important that the child comes up with the answers all by himself/herself.

5 Reasons to Adopt a Dog

5 reasons to adopt a dog	5 reasons not to adopt a dog
Ex. A dog will keep us more active.	Ex. The dog needs to go out, even when you don't want to.
1.	1.
2.	2.
3.	3.
4.	4.
5.	5.

Chapter 2:

Pixel

Gary and I met in London in 2003.

We fell in love, moved in together and he proposed to me during a holiday in Tokyo, Japan, in 2005. On a boiling day in June 2006, we got married in Switzerland and we had the most amazing day, surrounded by people we loved and couldn't have been happier.

Just before our wedding, I had qualified as a CELTA Teacher at the International House in London and I was teaching English to foreign students at a University Camp in the centre of London, Goodge Street. The kids were amazing, and I really loved teaching them.

Because I had been in their position and had similar experiences, I could easily relate to how they might have felt, and with the challenges of learning a foreign language, being in a foreign country, and feeling, at times, a little out of place. Also, I enjoyed the classroom feeling and seeing the children and felt a great sense of reward seeing the young adults I was working with grow and develop.

However, I had never forgotten how much Gary and I loved our time in Japan. Both of us were willing to try to move to Tokyo and experience life there.

Admittedly, I was far more willing to move to Japan than Gary was, so I actively searched for a job over there as an English teacher and found it fairly quickly.

I had to pass a first application, a test, and two interviews, but I survived the process and was offered the position as part of the JET (Japan Exchange and Teaching) Programme in Tokyo.

The school was in Ueno, which is a lovely district in Japan's capital, Tokyo. My new employment came with a package that included accommodation that was suitable for Gary and me to share; they were also going to provide health care and a reasonable salary. But when the process for the Visa started, they realised they couldn't offer accommodation and health care because I was Swiss and not English - if only they had looked at my CV sooner, they would have known that before putting me through such a gruesome process.

They could still offer me the position and salary, but everything else was up to me and Gary and, with that many uncertainties, we decided not to move there after all.

However, all the plans were in place and we both had resigned from our jobs in London, so we decided to move to Switzerland and give my hometown, Lugano, a try.

I wasn't as excited about moving back to Switzerland as I had been about moving to Japan until we realised Gary would work from home, I would teach in schools, and we could finally adopt a dog!

I had admired Pugs for a long time. The various pugs I met over the years had always been lovely and sweet, so we contacted a reputable breeder in the French part of Switzerland, who told us a litter was due just as we were moving into the country.

Our puppy would have then been ready for his new home that November, at 12 weeks old, which at the time was the age that breeders would allow puppies to be adopted in Switzerland.

Mrs. Perret lived in the town of Yvorne and had been breeding Pugs for a very long time. She had a wonderful reputation and was a properly registered breeder, which means that she was registered by the Kennel Club, but more importantly, she was known by local vets - yes, we asked more than one! In fact, she came recommended even by the vet we were going to take our future puppy to in the Italian part of Switzerland, which was a very good sign.

Every dog can have health issues, regardless of the breed, however, Pugs are flat-faced dogs (also called brachycephalic), which come with a whole set of health problems, such as breathing, digestive issues, eye diseases, and more.

At the time, I must admit, I didn't know anything about these issues. All I wanted was a Pug. I would have helped our doggy to overcome any potential health problems and I was sure I wasn't doing anything wrong by adopting a dog of that particular breed because I was going to love him more than life.

However, I am incredibly glad that we asked around and found a reputable breeder, because Mrs. Perret bred, as far as Pugs go, fairly healthy dogs for the time.

Yes, the nose could have been a little longer and thankfully over the years, I have noticed more slightly longer-faced Pugs. However, there are still many health issues within the breed that compromise their welfare.

At the end of the summer in 2006 was the very first time that we visited Mrs. Perret and the litter of 3 pups. The puppies were 5 weeks old and ready to meet humans outside the household.

I vividly remember walking into Mrs. Perret's house, into her open space kitchen, and seeing this massive playpen where Pepsi, the mum, was taking a nap. The 3 little puppies, all brothers, were cuddled up together. As we walked in, Pepsi looked up and the puppies ran along the side of the playpen to see what was happening.

Never, in my whole life, had I seen such a cute image.

The puppies were all apricot in colour, and their muzzles were a very dark brown, almost black, but not quite. They were a mixture of excited and wary and they all were of different sizes, from a chunky one to a smaller one, but they all seemed healthy.

Mrs. Perret told us one of the puppies was already spoken for, but we could choose which one we wanted to adopt from the other two.

We stayed there for a very long time, watching and interacting with the puppies and talking to Mrs. Perret. Between my broken French and her broken English, the hours flew by.

While we were there, one of the puppies pooed in their water (which Mrs. Perret took care of immediately), they had naps, played with each other, and ate a little, too. They were all absolutely adorable and goofy, but one of them stood out, especially to Gary. This little puppy was playing with Gary more than the others and, while interacting with him, he even worked out a little enrichment toy that was attached to the pen. Gary was smitten by the little guy and was really hoping we could adopt him. Of course, that puppy was the one already spoken for. We had no choice but to pick our second favourite, which was super friendly too and cute to the moon and back, of course, but I couldn't help thinking that Gary in particular, had started to build a bond with the other puppy, which was a real shame.

We left Mrs. Perret with the agreement to come back for two future visits. One in a few weeks to see the puppies again and then the second visit was in November to pick up our fluffy boy. We took time to reflect on and discuss our future plans as we drove the 4-hour journey back to Lugano, where we were going to move to at the end of that summer from the UK.

A couple of days after our visit, I received an email from Mrs. Perret who had also noticed how sweet the interaction between Gary and the puppy was. Very kindly, she had contacted the family who had chosen our favourite puppy before us, and they were happy for us to have him instead. I was impressed by the understanding Mrs. Perret had for the bond Gary had already started to form with the puppy and I could see why she was so highly recommended.

We were also happy to have chosen a name for our little boy, he was to be called Pixel. This was because Gary was a pixel artist and we felt it was the perfect name.

After all, an image missing a pixel is incomplete and, somehow, wrong. This is how we saw our little family: incomplete without our puppy.

At the end of that August, we had just moved from London to Lugano and were full of excitement and joy at the thought of seeing Pixel and his siblings again. We got into my little Smart Car, set up the GPS, and off we went. The drive was long, and once we passed the Gotthard Tunnel, which connects the Italian part of Switzerland to the German one, we were surprised to find snow! A lot, a lot of snow! And there was more coming!

At times, we had to stop by the side of the road because the snow was too bad, we couldn't even see where we were going. I am a confident driver, and so is Gary, but we were both rather scared to carry on. We had to make the difficult decision of turning back and giving up on seeing our boy that day. Not only were the roads and driving conditions bad, but I don't think my Smart car would have been up for such a challenging drive.

I can't begin to express how disappointed we both were.

Mrs. Perret, ever the kindest soul, sent us a lot of pictures of Pixel in the weeks after that until the day to pick him up came. By that time, we had found a flat by the idyllic Lake Lugano and had just moved in. We had bought a dog bed, 2 bowls, lots of toys, puppy pads, a lead, and a collar, and the food Mrs. Perret was feeding Pixel so that he would have the same food that he was used to. Everything was ready for him, although most of the things we thought we needed, we never used. Some of the things we thought that Pixel needed were wrong and we ended up throwing them away and buying the right ones. But, at the time, we didn't know what was right or wrong for dogs and we thought we were purchasing every item for our future puppy correctly.

One special day in November, we borrowed my parents' car, which was big and good on snow. This time, nothing was going to stop us from getting to Pixel and, indeed, nothing did!

We got to Yvorne without any problems, and our little boy came running into the big open kitchen when Mrs. Perret called him. He licked my hands and enjoyed cuddles with both Gary and I. After signing all the documents and saying our goodbyes to Mrs. Perret and all her other gorgeous pugs, we left. I will never forget saying goodbye to Pepsi, Pixel's mum. She looked up at me as if to say that it was ok for me to have one of her puppies. I hope she knew I was going to be the best mother I could be for him and that I already loved him with all my heart.

Key Points

<u>Choose your dog wisely</u>, I really cannot stress this enough.

When you decide to bring a dog into your life, many people might tell you to do your research first, and I hope you take on such great advice. This part is to help you to look at all aspects of such an important decision.

The very first thing you want to consider and look into is the **breed** of dog you are going to adopt and to do so, you need to look at your lifestyle and how the dog will fit into it.

You need to ask yourself the following questions:

- Are you and your family extremely active?
- Or are you more of the sedentary type?
- Do you work long hours away from home?
- Do you work from home and always around?
- Do you have children?
- If not, do you have friends or family with children visiting (often)?
- If you have kids, do you only have one child, or is your family a rather large one?
- Are your children all very young, or are they in their teens?
- Is <u>everyone</u> in the family on board and keen on adopting a dog?

Look at your environment and think about how a dog would fit into it:

- Do you live in a city or somewhere rural?
- Do you live in a house?
- Or do you live in a flat?
- Do you have a garden, no garden, shared garden? And how big is it? Is it fenced and secured?
- Do you have other pets? Would the existing pets be ok with you bringing a dog in?

Once you have honestly answered those questions, then you select a few breeds that match your lifestyle, environment, and family. Amongst those breeds, I am confident you will find the ones that **appeal** to you. I am saying this because, while all dogs, to me, are adorable and super cute, I know some are more appealing than others. I was smitten by Pugs years ago, although now I am keener on other breeds. Life changes, and you change with it.

Then you should look at the **temperament** of breeds, as some breeds of dogs tend to be, generally speaking, more friendly or more protective or more lazy or more active, you get the gist.

If your family is very active, then a dog from the working breeds might suit your lifestyle, like a working Cocker Spaniel, or a Labrador; but if you are more sedentary, perhaps a calmer breed would be best suited, like a Greyhound or a Newfoundland.

The general **health** of the breed should also be considered. As mentioned before, flat-faced dogs, such as Pugs, English Bulldogs, French Bulldogs, Boxers, etc. are prone to breathing problems, digestive issues, eye diseases, and more. So, have a look at the general health problems of the breeds that you are considering.

Another factor to consider is the **financial** one. Dogs cost money! And I am not only talking about the cost of the dog himself, which can be rather high sometimes, but I am talking about a lifetime commitment to your dog such as food, vet bills, harness, leads, training, walking, holiday time, silly little buys and things the dog might destroy as he learns not to.

On average, on food alone, people spend from £325 to £1,170 a year on their dog (Rover statistic, 2023).

According to the PDSA website, in 2022, the cost of a dog throughout their life (depending on their size) is estimated as:

- small dog would cost from £5,000 to £9,600
- medium dog breed costs between £6,600 and £10,400
- and a large dog can cost anything between £5,400 and £12,200

The calculations above are done on healthy dogs, so any illness or accident would increase the costs much more.

Pet **insurance** is always recommended, which can also be costly, but worth it, as vet bills can be incredibly expensive.

Grooming is another expense to consider. Some breeds of dogs will need more grooming requirements than others, but all dogs need regular husbandry care, which can be costly.

Once you have all the facts, pick your **breeder** well! Do your research and not only on Google. Your local vets, local qualified dog trainers/behaviourists, and even get in touch with groomers. See who they recommend and, if the same breeder gets mentioned lots of times, that's a good sign. Then, investigate their suggested breeders online. Can you find them on social media? They probably are on it! Check who comments on their posts, get in touch with people who have already adopted dogs from them, and ask them for feedback. Read reviews and when you connect with the breeder, don't be afraid to ask questions. I am sure that they will have plenty of questions for you too. It is, after all, an exchange. In fact, most good breeders, nowadays, ask for personal and professional references, which I think is brilliant and fair.

Finally, but certainly not the last thing to consider, is **training**! I know you might think I am biased, as I am a dog trainer and behaviourist, but I have always valued training, even before I was one myself.

Training is important to help you bond with your dog

and, even more importantly, to understand how we can guide our dogs in the crazy world of humans. How we can positively teach him what we want, while also respecting his needs.

I highly recommend getting in touch with a KAD Approved Professional, as they specialise in working with both small humans and dogs and they are all positive professionals, so you know no harm will come to your dog. See if there are any KAD Approved Professionals in your area:

www.kidsarounddogs.co.uk

What about rescuing a dog, you might ask?

Well, it is just the same, but different.

You might not be able to do much research on the breed, as many rescue dogs are of unknown breeds or are mixed breeds. Having said that, this can also be the case when adopting a puppy from a hobby breeder, for example.

In some cases, you might not get much on the history of the dogs, but you can still research the rescue centre the dog is at, and you should definitely ask about the health and temperament of the dog. A good rescue centre would have done a proper and professional temperament test and would have had the dog checked properly by a vet, which you are entitled to call to ask for advice. The same goes for the professional behaviourist that would have assessed the dog.

If anything is suspicious or 'doesn't feel right', do not adopt the dog. If something doesn't sound legally right, report it to the RSPCA or local authorities.

If you have children in the family, please do not adopt blindly. By this, I mean do not adopt without having had the chance to have the dog meet your children on multiple visits before adopting.

If the dog is from an overseas rescue, you also have to consider that the journey from another country to yours can be very traumatic for a dog and, sometimes, that trauma can change their personality. The new environment can also change their behaviour.

Going from living in a kennel with dogs, where they have barely any human interaction to a household full of kids is a very big change, that not many dogs (or people) can adapt to.

Remember to never put your children at risk with the dog you've chosen. And, if things don't work out, it's ok if you have no other choice but to have the dog rehomed.

When a dog is adopted from abroad, he will not go back to the adoption centre you got him from. It would be too much work and too costly, so you would have to find a local shelter for your dog and, as things are right now, not many rescue centres have the space for more dogs, so it wouldn't be as 'easy' as you might think.

All these factors can also have repercussions on how you raise your children and their safety, so please, think wisely before adopting a dog, whether from a reputable breeder or a rescue centre.

Chapter 3:

When Your Puppy is Your Baby

Pixel was my first-born child. You might laugh at this statement, but it was true then and, in my heart, it is still true today.

I had become a doggy-mum, and I loved it!

We lived in an apartment at the time, so toilet training was a little challenging and it took Pixel a good 6 to 8 months to really get it, but we did it!

It was simply a matter of really keeping an eye on him, making sure to take him outside every 45 minutes to 1 hour at first and getting up at night when needed.

I will be honest, I initially thought toilet training would have been easier, but, looking back, I can see the innocent mistakes we made, like taking him out but not always watching whether he was going to the toilet or just sniffing for fun.

Sometimes he would pretend to wee and then come up to me as if he'd done it to get his reward and, admittedly, I gave it to him, as I wasn't paying enough attention. I know it was the same for Gary. In other words, our pug was cleverer than us!

Another mistake was letting too much time pass before taking him out, and so he would go toilet in the house.

I would also often misplace the harness and/or the lead, and I would waste time looking for it. Pugs wait for no man, so he would simply wee inside.

A big rule is also to pop your dog out after a meal, which might have been overlooked at times and when that happened, you guessed it, Pixel would go toilet indoors.

We also tried to use puppy pads, because that's what the sales assistant in the shop told us we were going to need, so we followed that advice. However, Pixel would either try to chew the pads or seemed to purposely miss them.

In a short amount of time, I understood that the pads might have been good firmly secured in a playpen or crate, so the dog couldn't chew the corners. However, we only had an open room and no playpen or crate. Gary and I would have had to cover the entire floor in pee pads for Pixel to learn not to pee on the floor, then remove one pee pad at a time. But this was entirely unfeasible, costly and bad for the environment. It seemed all silly and pointless.

So, we packed up the rest of the pee pads and donated them to a local charity instead.

The more I think about the times we were toilet training Pixel, the more I see how all his incidents were always our fault… whether we were distracted, forgetful, lazy or tired, every little wee done indoors by our puppy was because of us, not him.

This is another reason why we never, ever told him off for our mistakes!

At the time we also started a puppy class in a nearby town. The trainer took pride in having years of experience working with dogs, while Gary and I were first-time dog caregivers, so we went to the classes, hoping to learn about our dog and how to raise Pixel properly and with loving care.

However, very little of what that man told us resonated with Gary or I. We were given outdated advice that neither of us were going to follow, such as:

If Pixel went toilet in the house, the guy told us to put Pixel's face on the wee, so he would know not to do it; or to tap him on the nose with a newspaper.

The man also told us that our puppy wasn't fully listening to us because he did not see us as his 'superiors' (alpha) and we had to assert our place in our puppy's life.

So, he taught us to get our puppy to roll his belly and hold him down. That position is called the Alpha Roll.

When we got home, I went online to search for that term and other people seemed to believe in it, so I admit, I tried it.

And I hated it!

Pixel's belly was round, cute and warm. I wanted to just tickle it, but instead I was holding it down because I thought that was what I was supposed to do. In his extreme stress, my little boy was struggling and tried to bite my hand, which he couldn't reach.

Gary walked into the room and saw us in that position. He saw how worried and upset I looked and how distressed Pixel was.

'This can't be right.' he said.

'It doesn't feel right, but that's what the guy told us to do. I am not sure at all, though.' I replied.

'I think we should look into it a bit more.' Gary suggested.

I happily released my puppy from that awful position and profusely apologized to him for keeping him pinned to the floor. 'It won't happen again.' I promised him.

We never went back to that so-called trainer and bought a book called 'It's Me or The Dog' by the wonderful Victoria Stillwell. We also downloaded her TV show by the same name as the book and learnt from that as much as we could.

At the time, online dog training wasn't a thing, so there was nothing of that kind. I wanted to find a force-free trainer, as those are professionals who don't punish the dog for getting stuff wrong. Force-free dog trainers don't use hurt, shout, or use tools that could harm dogs in anyway, and that was (and still is) my style. However, we were struggling to find a force-free qualified trainer in Switzerland or Italy. We lived so close to the North of Italy, I wouldn't have minded the drive, if it meant training my puppy right. So, a lot of the things we were learning were from books inspired by the Victoria Stillwell one, which were as kind as dog training got back then.

Victoria Stillwell was a bit of a revolution to dog training in households back then, after known TV shows freely presented harsher ways to train dogs. Victoria, although still not as good and positive as she is today, was on the path of helping dogs positively, which is what we wanted too.

Luckily for us, it was just Gary and I, so we had the space and time to raise Pixel in a way that it wouldn't be stressful, unfair, or unethical. Pixel didn't have any behavioural issues that we could see, and all we needed was basic training, so, in some ways, we had 'room for error', because we were not feeling any kind of pressure.

We also quickly learned that collars weren't good for pugs, and, in time, I learned they aren't good for any dog.

Pugs have a big neck, especially male ones, so effectively, their head is smaller than their neck and collars easily slip out, leaving the dog off lead and, potentially, unsafe. Moreover, when Pixel would pull on the lead, the collar would put pressure on his neck and he would often struggle to breathe because of that, which would cause him to make some choking noises and cough. We didn't feel right about it and, after researching other options, we liked the look of harnesses, which go around the whole body of the dog so, even if he were to pull, the pressure would be spread out on his chest and girth, giving him no pain and still allowing him to breathe!

At the time, we were also using an extendable lead, also called a flexi-lead. Basically, we would attach the lead to Pixel's harness and the rest would roll in a plastic box, which we could control with a button. So, if Pixel needed more lead, we would click the button and release more of it, if he needed less lead, we would have to call him to us, so the lead would loosen and, by pressing the button, it would get back in the plastic box.

Some days it was like playing yo-yo with the Pug!

One day, I was sitting by the lake with Pixel. I was reading a book, enjoying the warmth of spring. I had shorts on, and Pixel was resting under the bench. It was a lovely thing that we did every so often.

Suddenly, a little dog came by to give Pixel a sniff and then moved away. As the dog left, Pixel got up to follow him, but my left leg was tangled in the extendable lead. I couldn't shorten the lead, because Pixel was pulling towards the dog, and my leg was in the way. The more he pulled, the more the lead was digging into me. It was atrociously painful! Luckily, Pixel responded to my distressed voice and little scream of pain, so he came back to me, and I managed to get my leg untangled. The lead had effectively burned my skin and there was a very red, hideous, and very painful mark on my shin.

I hopped home in tears and Gary took me to a pharmacy, where I was given a cream and a look of sympathy.

As soon as I could, I bought a normal lead and stayed away from the retractable one whenever I could. Because people loved them so much, I felt it was my fault that I got hurt and that I was basically a bit of an idiot and that's why it happened, so I didn't insist on throwing it away. I simply didn't want to use it anymore and, once it eventually broke, I was rather happy and never bought another one again.

Gary taught Pixel a lot of cute tricks, like giving paw, sit, spin and others that, now, I fail to recall. They had more time at home together, as I was teaching a lot, but Pixel loved me so, so much and if he had any preference between Gary and me, he'd never shown it.

He loved us equally. I believe that to this day.

Gary and I both believed we were good parents to Pixel and, while he was our whole world, we also felt we were ready for a human child in our life.

But who knew that getting pregnant was that difficult?

Key Points

Training!
Positive reinforcement, also called Force Free training, means that we don't hurt dogs, we don't shout at dogs, and we don't use any tools that can hurt dogs, physically or emotionally.

If things don't go as planned, stop and take a look at the environment to see if there is anything too distracting or even stressful for your dog. These factors make it very difficult for dogs to concentrate on you and what you want them to do.

Observe the actual situation, such as what the triggers were and how they could be avoided in the future. Often it helps to go somewhere different and quieter that is less exciting or distracting to your dogs, bearing in mind that every dog is different and what one might find interesting, another might not.

Don't underestimate the importance of your dog's health, because being unwell, injured, or in pain can stress, upset and/or anger our dogs.

What about the rewards you are using? Are they enticing enough to counter the distractions? They might not be, so you ought to up your game and make the rewards the best they can be. Go for things like hotdogs, chicken, ham and so on. All cut up very small, think pea-sized!

Ask yourself what you could have done differently to help your dog not to react the way that they did and how you could have prevented a mistake from happening: how you can help your dog achieve success instead.

Always reward your dog when they show right or appropriate behaviours! Reward your dogs with food, or toys or cuddles or other things they might want that you know they enjoy.

It is important to know what your dog considers to be a reward, not what you think might be good for our dogs. For example, if I work with a dog that doesn't like to be petted that much, giving him a cuddle would stress him, not make him happy. If, instead, I was to give that dog a ball, which is his favourite toy, the dog might really appreciate it and consider that an awesome reward for responding to me so well.

Be your dog's advocate: if something doesn't feel right, take your dog away from that situation.

Most of all, always remember to be patient and not to expect too much too soon. You know what they say, 'Rome wasn't built in a day' and 'Good things come to those who wait'. Those are all great quotes to keep in mind when training dogs and raising kids!

I strongly believe that it is always best to work with a qualified dog trainer or behaviourist, as they will be able to help you on a personal level, recognising your dog's needs, wants, strengths and weaknesses; to then give you and your dogs the best possible support to create and keep a wonderful bond that will last a lifetime!

All Kids Around Dogs® Professionals are qualified to help you achieve just that, and you can find your local KAD® Approved Professional in the directory of our website.

Every family and every dog is different, but here is a list of the most common and basic behaviours dogs who share a life with kids might need and why.

Respond to name: it's very important for a dog to know his name for everyday life moments. Your main goal here is that he can listen and respond to the person who calls him. For example, say you might want to take a photo of your dog or you might want to distract him from a situation that may lead him into trouble, including jumping up at guests, or picking up something off the floor.

Down: I find this behaviour particularly useful with big dogs, as by laying down, they reduce their size quite a bit, making it less intimidating for little children. However, the most useful reason for you to train your dog the 'down', is to prevent your dog jumping up at people. This, of course, can also be prevented by having your dog on a lead, whether in the house or outside. Keeping your dog on the lead is management, which is key when training dogs.

Wait: dogs can be so easily excited by life that they are impatient. Teach them to wait for their own safety throughout their life! Such as before getting their meals, before opening the boot of the car at the park, before letting them free to play, or before opening your house door, and so much more.

Touch: I love this behaviour, which is when the dog touches your hand (or another part of your body) with his nose. I use 'touch' so much! It is a great form of 'recall', it's a great way to get your dog to 'leave' something or someone alone, it is also a brilliant way for your dog to let you know he needs something, by poking your with his nose, rather than perhaps bark at you, or scratching your leg with his paws, which are all behaviours that can scratch children, hurting them.

Walk nicely on the lead: whether you have a small dog or a big one, I am pretty sure you want your walks with your dog to be enjoyable, and you don't want your dog to pull you down the road, or to walk all over the place, as if you were both drunk. Moreover, when a dog walks nicely on the lead, it is also a sign the dog is relaxed and quite content to be out and about, rather than stressed, overexcited or unhappy.

The behaviours listed and explained are what I would teach to all my clients, whether or not they had children, simply because they are all important for dogs to know and to respond to when living in a polite society. Society that, regardless of the dog's family situation, will most definitely include children of all ages.

As you can see, I like to keep things simple when it comes to essentials. Training is fun and important for both humans and dogs, so I work on more things to teach my dogs and my clients. However, what to train and teach our dogs and their caregivers is mostly down to the lifestyle, needs and opportunities they have. Especially the dog.

Chapter 4:

Adoption Around Dogs

Ever since I was a little girl playing with dolls, I always imagined I would have only one child and this child would be a girl.

How I would name this imaginary child varied a lot, but the idea was always the same… I was to have a little girl.

Funny thing is, nobody actually tells you it isn't that easy to get pregnant in the first place. Getting a baby to 'stick' isn't like in the movies… and after 3 years of trying, 3 years of getting disappointed every month, I was ready to give up on the little girl that I had always dreamed of having.

I could have gone to the doctor and tried to find out why I wasn't getting pregnant, and whose 'fault' it was. But that's the thing I didn't want to know. What if it was me? I would have felt so guilty about myself… and what if it was Gary? He would have felt terrible! We didn't want that for us.

The idea of adopting also crossed our mind, but I wasn't sure I was ready to go down that path, which is a very challenging one. Inspections, finance, so much scrutinising, and there was never a guarantee we could have been chosen.

Adopting, in my opinion, is an even bigger decision than having a child naturally.

However, even if adopting a child has not been my personal experience, I would like to dedicate some words about it, because many wonderful families with dogs adopt children and I feel they ought to know a little about what to expect when that is their journey.

In the UK, there isn't a specific department that deals with families who have dogs in their home and are planning on adopting a child. In fact, the social work practitioner in charge of that specific case or family will also be the one assessing the dog/s in the household. And, while social workers do an amazing job, they are not dog professionals, so they don't know about dogs' body language, dog behaviours and what to expect a dog to do and not to do. They might have an idea of what a dog should and shouldn't do, but that isn't the same for every dog, moreover, some behaviours are misunderstood, or fairly easy to work with, so a family would have all the chances of being approved after some dog training lessons. Similarly, a dog might react mildly negatively towards something happening in their surroundings, which is missed, but that behaviour might reappear and perhaps even stronger once a child joins the family.

Some social workers, who are a bit more pro-active or unsure about dogs, would get in touch with a qualified dog behaviourist to assess the dog in an appropriate and professional way, which, in my opinion, should always be the way, regardless of the dog, the family and the adoption agency used.

Another important factor to consider when adopting a child is the age and history of the child. If the child is a baby or a toddler, chances are that, despite their upbringing up until that point, the children might act just like any other little child would. However, if the child was a little older and with a difficult background, the family should be informed as to whether there were dogs in the previous household and how they were treated. A child witnessing their parents being abusive towards animals might believe that is the way to treat dogs. They might not know any better and, therefore, feel they should do the same with the new dog they meet and live with.

There could be deeper and even more upsetting things children might do around and to the dogs, simply because they haven't been shown, don't know how else to live with an animal, or they are too traumatized by what they saw, and the dog becomes their emotional 'dumping ground'. Sometimes dogs can be great for emotional support if the child knows to be gentle with dogs, but sometimes if the child has seen people abuse dogs, then they might negatively and with physical force, project their trauma onto the dog.

If the child comes from a difficult background, where dogs were involved, and possibly even seized by the authorities, this information needs to be known by the adopting family and the person assessing the dog, as it might not be beneficial to have a dog in a household with that particular child.

When a dog is assessed with child-adoption in mind, some basic things need to be considered:

The dog needs to be friendly with known people and strangers.

As the child will be new to the family, and social workers will pay visits from time to time to make sure things are working out ok. The child might also have to see a therapist, or similar who does home visits.

There might be teachers doing home-visits; the child will hopefully make new friends, who will visit the house where the dog lives.

If the dog doesn't want other people in his home, you can see how this can be problematic.

However, we also don't want a dog to be too friendly such as wanting to exuberantly jump at visitors, or going up to every person he sees when out and about. Let's just say, you want the dog to be happy to share a world with humans, without being overly fussy about them.

For the reasons above, the dog needs to have a calm temperament. If you have an easily excitable dog in a prospective family, things may perhaps get even more challenging with a child in the home and might even make the child scared of dogs, even when the dog only means to have fun and play around.

It is essential that the dog doesn't show any resource guarding behaviours either. This means the dog doesn't want to protect things like food, water, toys, locations (from the whole house to a half-chewed toilet roll on the floor), people (his caregivers or other people around him), other objects, such as acting differently than normal if he has one of your socks and you want it back. This could be displayed with something as innocent as keeping a paw on the item that they find precious, to baring their teeth someone comes too close to the dog while the item is there too.

Don't worry, you don't need to have the perfect 'Disney' dog, but we need to make sure both the child joining your family and your dog can be happy and safe together, so the assessment from a dog professional would be far more in-depth and accurate.

Chapter 5:

Moving Back to the UK

Switzerland wasn't giving us joy at all. I worked at 3 different schools and was barely ever home, so Gary was alone with Pixel a lot. While Gary had his job, a great passion for video games, and Pixel was amazing company, I know Gary must have felt lonely. This wasn't what we signed up for, so at the beginning of summer 2010, we moved back to the UK.

It was a time before Brexit, so getting Pixel into the UK wasn't that difficult, and all his documents and vaccinations were in order and up to date. So, with the exception of the inevitable stress the journey must have caused him, everything else wasn't that challenging.

To get to the UK, we drove from Lugano to Calais, France, from where we got the train to Dover via the Eurotunnel. During our long drive, we took a break by spending one night in a hotel in the middle of France.

Finding hotels that allow dogs in France was fairly easy, but I wonder if they expected him to sleep on the bed with us. Probably not! But they shall never know that's what happened!

In our case, the hotel was a temporary stay, so Pixel had to try to relax in the new room with all these unfamiliar smells and feels after being in a car for hours.

When we stayed in the hotel that night, did he think it was going to be forever? I wonder...

Then we had another day of driving, the stress of the Eurotunnel, the various noises, lights, smells, you name it!

When we arrived at the Eurotunnel, we found it really well organised and super easy to find.

We parked at the massive station, then got Pixel and his travel documents (also known as pet passports) checked. The staff barely even looked at Pixel, but took the documents and stamped them before giving them back, and off we went.

The train was hot and, while we were allowed to get out of the car, it was only to stand around our vehicle and nothing else. It wasn't very well lit, and it was somewhat noisy. Worried about how this might make Pixel feel, I sat at the back with him and gave him some cuddles.

We had packed some sandwiches, which we happily shared with our little pug. If I remember correctly, the journey in the tunnel was about an hour. Once we got to Dover, getting out and on the road was quick and easy and as we had already dealt with the travel pet screening before the tunnel, no one needed to check Pixel's documents. Since Brexit, we haven't taken any of our dogs on a trip of this kind. From my understanding, things have got much trickier about travelling into the UK with dogs originating outside the UK.

I think, overall, Pixel handled the long drive very well. We made sure to stop every hour or so to just stretch our legs and his paws. Also, this helped us to feel refreshed, considering that we both were driving a long distance, which can be very tiring. So, you can imagine how nice it was for us to finally arrive at Gary's parents, in London, after two days of travelling.

My parents-in-law, John and Christine, and Gary's sister Charlotte, lived in the North of London, in the house Gary grew up in and that I was also familiar with. However, to Pixel, everything was new and, while he was loved there, had a great garden to play in, and Gary's family was super nice to him and looked after him very well, the novelty and unfamiliarity of the place must have been a little confusing to him. Not to mention that he was sharing the garden with Thomas the Tortoise, which was a new friend to make.

Thomas was lovely (and still is) and would let Pixel sniff his garden as much as he wanted, but we had to be very careful with the food Thomas had, as tortoises can have things like grapes, which are poisonous for dogs. We had all these extra and new little things to consider that we never had to think about before.

After that first month, we moved Pixel again, into our lovely flat in Bournemouth. I am sure he thought my in-laws' house was his new home! Imagine how confusing it must have been for him to be moved again!

He truly was a wonderful dog and endured it all amazingly well, but all that moving around and all those changes are very stressful. If you are moving home, this is something to be mindful of.

For about a month or so we stayed at Gary's parents', until we found the perfect place to move into in Bournemouth, Dorset.

We had chosen Dorset as a location for our home because Gary's brother, Mark lived there with his wife Marianne and their two boys, Alex and Oliver (now they also have a little girl, Katie).

Moreover, Dorset is beautiful! The beaches with their gorgeous clear sand and not far from it, the national park New Forest as well as many parks and places to visit.

Both Gary and I felt that there was nothing missing in this county, and we were very happy to move there, with our furry child, Pixel, of course.

Once again, we moved into a flat, so no garden for us, but we lived right next to Queens Park, a massive park where people often go and walk their dogs. Pixel loved it, even if it was also a golf club, so we had to be mindful while walking around that we wouldn't get hit by a flying golf ball, which luckily never happened!

It didn't take me long to find a job as an English teacher in a school near our place, in Charminster. The school was small, but could guarantee me classes every morning, 5 days a week, and some private lessons in the afternoon.

I was working much less than I did when in Switzerland, but the cost of living in the UK was also very different than Switzerland, which meant we were financially ok, even with less income from my part.

This also meant I had more time to spend with Pixel. We would take long walks together, or he would sit with me while I'd prepare my lessons. I also made friends with a lovely pug-lady also called Debbie and we would sometimes meet up for coffee or walks. Her pugs were super cute and funny, and she was a pleasure to be with.

Moreover, I had the opportunity to get closer to my sister-in-law Marianne, since they didn't live far from us, so I enjoyed spending some time with her and my gorgeous nephews, Alex and Oliver. Alex was about to turn 3 when we moved to Dorset and Oliver was just a toddler, barely over a year old. Both boys weren't strangers to dogs, as Marianne's parents had dogs, horses and even a cat, which led their whole family to help the children understand that they had to respect dogs and all animals. But, more importantly at that age, is the fact that dogs were not a novelty to them as they were so used to seeing them around. Having the constant exposure and experiences around dogs meant that neither of the kids felt the need to always approach Pixel, when they were over at our place.

Pixel was also welcome at their house, which we really appreciated.

I think both Mark and Marianne knew that we considered Pixel as our child. They had Alex and Oliver, while we had Pixel. In fact, if I think about it again, I think most of our family and friends had stopped asking us about when we were going to have a baby and had just settled with Pixel being our child.

Once settled in our flat, the new job and our new life in Bournemouth, Gary went to visit his parents in London while I stayed behind with Pixel to have some 'me time' (when your husband works from home, you don't get much time for yourself). It was that weekend that I realized I was feeling a little 'different'.

The signs were mostly coming from Pixel, who had been exceptionally cuddly: his head seemed to constantly be on my tummy, and he had also taken to following me around, which a lot of dogs do, but he wasn't generally like that.

Somehow, he seemed different, more attached to me, more caring.

That, and the fact that I was 'late' somehow gave me a little hope, but I wasn't getting too excited about anything just yet. After 3 years of disappointments trying to get pregnant, I had developed thicker skin, and I didn't want my heart to take over my brain.

So, I spent a good part of that weekend looking for pug breeders in England and even getting in touch with some of them, with the idea of adopting another dog, who would have been Pixel's sibling and would have made Gary and I parents again, in our own way.

My thinking at the time was that looking for a puppy and possibly adopting one was easy. In fact, it didn't take me long to find a few breeders and to get in touch with them. It would have been very easy to schedule to see the puppies when ready, and, eventually, choose the puppy we wanted and complete the adoption. All those things could be planned and were certain, but getting pregnant was so difficult for me. For those 3 years, finding out that I wasn't pregnant was heartbreaking every time.

I couldn't do it anymore.

However, when Gary came back from his trip to London, as the Autumn leaves had started to fall, we found out that we were expecting.

All the signs Pixel was giving me were found. For the first time, my gut instincts were right. 5 pregnancy tests I took, all positively telling us a baby was growing inside of me, were not wrong. Few things in life gave me that much joy.

As I called my mother to give her the news, I just knew I would finally have the baby girl I dreamed of for so long.

Key Points

Life-changing events, such as moving home, are stressful for all involved. However, us humans can rationalise it. We know certain steps need to be taken; we know why we are moving, where we are going, we'd have a schedule in place, and so on.

However, dogs don't have that luxury! Dogs just see stuff getting packed, things taken away, smells being all over the place, just like our emotions and stress-levels.

When dogs get moved from their home, possibly the only home they have known for years, to a new place, it smells different; it looks different; it feels different. And they don't even understand why they are there.

What you can do to reduce stress for your dog when you move:

Take it easy, give your dog plenty of sniffing time, get him to play easy sniffing-games. My favourite is not technically a game, but for the dog it would be, which is Freework!

Animal Behaviourist and one of my idols, Sarah Fisher, founded the association Animal Centred Education (ACE), which is where, amongst other things, you can professionally learn about Freework. You can check out ACE and Freework at their website listed at the end of the book.

However, Freework can also be done in a more informal manner by placing treats in, on and around items in your house, or bits of recycling materials, such as boxes or bottles or old furniture. You can create an easy or trickier course for your dog and hide treats around it. Use spreadable stuff, like pate or spreadable cheese on those items. Then, release the dog and let him find all those hidden treasures.

The 'finding' part of Freework means your dog will activate his sense of smell, using his powerful nose. By sniffing, he will also release calming signals to his brain, helping him to feel calmer, build confidence and self-esteem.

I also like a series of products from Pet Remedy. They use all natural elements, such as Valerian, Sweet Basil and Clary Sage essential oils, which help dogs by telling their nerve cells to calm down. In some dogs, the change is instant, in others, it takes longer.

I suggest you use Pet Remedy alongside an exercise like Freework. You could spray some Pet Remedy products in the room where your dog will be searching, or spray some items the dog will be smelling (a little will go a long way!). Just remember to never spray these products directly onto your dog. This is for two main reasons. The first one is that the dog might get scared and see being sprayed as a punishment, which would be very sad and upsetting.

The second reason is that if the spray is in the air, and not on the body of the dog, the dog has the choice and agency to leave the room, to avoid smelling an item that has been sprayed, or, more likely, the dog will choose to smell those items more. However, regardless of how much or little he wants to sniff the sprayed items, it would be his choice. But if the spray goes on his body, he won't be able to move away from it, taking away the sense of agency and increasing stress levels, defeating the purpose.

Finally, if you possibly can, get help! If you are only moving from one place to another, without moving country like we did, why not have a dog boarder help out? Your dog could go stay there while you are dealing with the stress of the move, and then pick him up and take him home when all the furniture and the rest is in place. Even just a couple of days to get your new place a little more sorted, without adding the stress of having your dog around, or the sense of guilt because everything is a mess and you don't have time to properly care for your dog, can be a godsend!

Make sure the dog boarder is someone you know, and that you can have a trial before your move.

Family members or friends might also be able to help you, don't be afraid to accept or ask for help. The help is not just for you, but for the love of your dog too.

Chapter 6:

Pregnancy Around Dogs

I should say this outright, I did not like being pregnant!

Everybody tells you how wonderful it is, and how you will glow and all that. Well, I can tell you that I was not glowing! My hair was dull, and my skin wasn't looking any better, despite taking all the suggested vitamins.

I quickly learned that morning sickness isn't just in the morning, so that did not make the first few months a lot of fun.

Also, my immune system was very low, because my body was so busy looking after the growing baby, so when I caught a really bad cold and I had a temperature, it made me feel like death was upon me as I couldn't take any medicines, only paracetamol, which didn't do much at all!

Throughout all those experiences, Pixel was always by my side. I was still working at the time, so he would be Gary's assistant in the mornings, and then glued to me for the rest of the day.

Just after Christmas, we had the best gift – we found out that we were going to have a girl. I remember when the nurse told us, I was happy, of course, but not surprised. I had willed for a baby girl for so long, she was always meant to be with us. When Spring arrived, and with our baby girl due in May, I started to feel a lot of pain in my pelvis. I couldn't walk unaided, I couldn't get out of bed, I couldn't even get in bed without Gary helping me. The baby was fine, but I had developed something called Pelvic Girdle Pain (PGP) or Symphysis Pubis Dysfunction (SPD).

It started with a little bit of pain, which made me worry the baby wasn't well, but the midwife reassured us she was fine, while diagnosing me with PGP. She also went on to inform me that there wasn't a cure for that, and it was due to the baby growing and pressing on that part of the body. She told us the pain will go away after giving birth, especially if by natural birth and not by C-section. She warned me not to take any other medicines other than Paracetamol to ease the pain, which to be honest, was pretty useless.

She also told me that the pain was likely to get worse throughout the course of the pregnancy, as our baby was growing and putting more and more pressure on my pelvis.

And, boy, was she right! The pain got so bad, I was even given crutches to walk with, which I hated so much! I felt like I was depending on someone else, mainly Gary, and I was losing myself completely.

I hated not being able to walk Pixel, as we had been enjoying our outings so much before that. In fact, I was sure that going out for walks with Pixel was reducing all the other symptoms. However, walking was incredibly painful, and as the pregnancy progressed, it was out of the question for me to walk without someone else with me. It also it simply wasn't safe for me to be alone, in case the pain stopped me all together.

I couldn't drive either, and taking the stairs to get to our flat was a challenge.

Anyway, I think you get the gist of how awful PGP was for me. This was something I had never heard of before it happened to me, but I have since learned that many women suffer with this pain during pregnancy. Some less than others, but it is not to be taken lightly.

However, I do believe everything happens for a reason, and getting PGP helped us prepare Pixel for the arrival of our baby girl, because I had to leave work on maternity leave sooner than expected; Gary had to take more care of me, the house and Pixel. Our outings together were limited and always a bit tricky.

We even had tickets to see The Decemberists in London and had to give them up because I couldn't sit in the car for that long to get there. I couldn't have sat or stood at the concert either, it would have been too long and too painful.

I had to give up on a few things during pregnancy due to PGP, but I am still so gutted about the concert, because The Decemberists is a band both Gary and I absolutely love.

So, you see, changing our lifestyle around PGP such as giving up on outings and trips away made us feel as if the baby had already arrived!

Pixel never had a proper routine, apart from having his breakfast around 7am and dinner around 4pm. We didn't have a set time for walks or other things, which I believe helped massively when things had to change.

With a new baby soon coming into the house, keeping a routine could have been a challenge and, while I admire all the super-organised families out there, I knew we were not going to be one of those.

Before PGP immobilised me, I had been the one mainly walking Pixel, but our little dog loved and adored Gary, so it wasn't an issue for him the fact that I wasn't always with them on walks. I also think he was enjoying more snuggle time with me.

A friend kindly bought me a nursing pillow, which is shaped to hold the baby during nursing. I knew I was going to use that a lot, so I made sure Pixel knew what it was, and he became familiar with it. The goal was for him to know the pillow was there, and not to chew on it or consider it as one of his toys.

However, I did leave it out often and found Pixel asleep curled up next to it or even on it.

Don't get me wrong, that was super cute, and I let him do it, but I really shouldn't have, because that way Pixel thought it was ok to sleep on the nursing pillow and associate it to something he could have and use, but when the baby was going to be there, I needed Pixel to know that it was the baby's pillow. Surely learning one thing and then the opposite could not have been good for him, and it would have confused him.

Back then, I didn't know this. I thought it was enough for him to know to be by my side when I was using it or pretend to be using it, but it didn't occur to me that I could confuse him when I wasn't around.

In the house, more and more new things started appearing such as a changing unit in the bathroom, a Moses basket, a cot, a pushchair, a car seat, boxes of nappies, baby wipes, toys... and a playpen.

We got him to sniff everything. I wanted him to get his curiosity 'out of the way', while it was safe and stress-free.

Every time he would move away from the new items, he would get rewarded. Often, I would hope he would move away by himself, without being told, but my impulse to ask him to 'leave' whatever he was interested in was too strong. So, more often than not, I would end up asking him to move away from random baby items. Now, I look back at those training sessions now thinking I really should have spoken less and trusted him more. The concept behind speaking less and letting my dog problem-solve was that if I was always telling my dog to 'leave' something alone, would he do it when I was not there?

What if I'd come back from an outing with my baby, take her to the crib or to get something and leave the car seat by the entrance? Pixel, with his natural curiosity, would want to investigate it. What would happen if I left the room with him there forgetting to ask Pixel to 'leave' the car seat alone? Perhaps, I would come back to it later with him having chewed some of it or more likely taking a nap in it? That's not what I wanted.

I wanted him to know that investigating things is ok, but it's even better when he steps away from them.

Training such cues can take some time, or very little time at all, but it is absolutely worth it and it really ought to be done before the baby arrives home.

Whether during pregnancy or while going through the adoption process, doing this kind of work ahead of time can save you so much trouble and stress.

Admittedly, we were lucky: Pixel was never that much of a chewer and barely ever destroyed stuff, like furniture or else. But when it came to the baby stuff, we were definitely more on edge for these than other items and I am sure Pixel could pick up on our feelings.

At home, Pixel never needed to be away from us and always had the run of the place, but a baby was soon to join our household, so things would have had to change.

Please, remember how much I loved Pixel and how important he was to me and my husband. We wanted him to really be a brother to our baby girl. We wanted them to become friends and to get on very well, but at the same time, we knew we had to prepare him for the big changes ahead. That way, at least one of us would have been ready, because I am not sure Gary and I really were – the thought of being new parents was scary!

To help manage our future life at home with Pixel and the baby, we placed a stairgate between the kitchen and the rest of the flat and purchased a playpen for the baby.

Pixel was still our furry child, but when he had his meal, the novel situation was that we would have the stairgate closed. So, we took time to get him used to that change.

We also placed the baby toys and other baby items in the playpen, while he still had access to the rest of the room. Again, this was to get him used to the new items and layout in the flat.

Finally, we started putting the lead on him randomly during the day around the home even when we weren't going out, so that he would get used to having it indoors too. This way he would understand that having the lead on wouldn't always mean an outing was coming.

We were ready for our baby girl to be born… or were we?

Key Points

Prepare ahead of time! The moment you find out that you are expecting you will likely have a few months to get the house and dog baby-proofed.

Stair gates, playpens or separate rooms can be your friends, as using them is also a form of management, which is key in training plans and real-life scenarios. Especially when babies and children are involved.

Your dog might not be used to being around the home in these areas without you while you are home, or being left alone, or to having a designated area for meals, resting or toys. This is why you need to take the time to help your dog happily adjust to all these changes.

Take a look at your house and ask yourself the following questions:

- Is there a place where your dog loves to stay the most?
- Are you going to feed your baby in the nursery all the time?
- Or are you likely to nurse on the sofa?
- If your baby is a great sleeper, things can be easier. But you need to mentally prepare and think that your child isn't going to sleep much when you want her to. Especially at first.

By working out which room and space you will be

using the most to nurse your baby, it is worth getting the dog to be somehow around you, so he knows he's not losing you to a new human child. Start by getting him used to a divider or the stairgate or any other item you'll use to keep the dog away during those times or when you feel the dog shouldn't interrupt you and the baby.

This is not about feeling like you are putting up a wall between you and the dog, but it is about safety and the need for space. For safety, of course, the first thought is about the dog reacting negatively towards the baby, like scratching the baby, or, worse, biting her. However, it is more than that. We don't know how the baby will affect our dog. We need to make plans to keep the dog happy even when we can't be there to help him be content and relaxed; and when the baby arrives, we will work to help positively introduce them and create good associations.

However, we can't be 100% sure that the dog will be ok with the baby at all times, just as we can't say for sure that the dog will hate having the baby around. It will depend on the work you do beforehand, and how the dog will feel each day, how much screaming the baby will do, the different smells, how tired you will be and so much more.

It is impossible to know exactly what your dog or your baby might do every moment of the day, so having a space for your dog to be, where he is happy and relaxed, is the best thing you can do to help your dog! That way, while you deal with your baby and the stress of it all, your dog won't add to your worries. Your dog will be fine where you have shown him to be, because all good things have been happening in there, including chilling and napping alone.

Don't forget that dogs have an extremely powerful nose and sense of smell, so you can use that to your advantage! We can get our dogs to associate a certain smell with a feeling or a reaction. Let me put this in a human situation for you. Say you love pizza, and you are hungry. The smell of tomato and melted mozzarella on dough would make you really want to have some, right?

What about the 'lemon test'? I want you to close your eyes and imagine a lemon! It's yellow, oval, and its skin it's slightly rough. Now, I want you to smell that lemon and really get into the citrus scent of the fruit. Now, I want you to imagine what it would taste like if you bite into the lemon! Can you taste the sourness? Did that make you close your eyes even more? Did that make your mouth pucker? Did you even shake your head? That's the power of our brain, that knows what the acidity of the lemon would do to us, even if we are not really biting into a lemon and it's all in our mind.

That's the same thing we can help our dogs to understand: your dog should learn to associate the smell of the baby with positive and calming things, like a gentle massage, scattered treats for him to sniff and find (emphasis on the sniffing part, which helps to calm a dog's mind), or having a nap.

You really don't want your dog to associate the baby with something to be excited or worried about.

If the dog thinks the baby is exciting, he will want to jump, run, play and just be bonkers around the baby. If the dog thinks the baby is worrisome, he will be scared, fearful and might either hide from the baby or, worse, feel like he needs to defend himself from her, which could lead to biting.

Now, I know you'll be wondering how you can prepare your dog ahead of time to associate positively towards the smell of the baby, when the baby hasn't born yet. Don't worry, you don't need your real baby, just what the baby is likely to smell of.

For example:

- The detergent you will be using to wash the baby's clothes.
- The wipes you'll use to wipe the baby's bottom, hands, etc.
- What about talcum powder?
- Nappies?
- What about when you will be disinfecting the baby bottle in boiling water or one of those new disinfection machines?
- Or perhaps you will be breastfeeding? Although, even when breastfeeding you will, occasionally, be using a bottle, so the smell of

disinfected bottles, among other items, will be in the air.

- All those smells, even the ones we, as mere humans, cannot smell, will be in the air and your dog, with his powerful nose, will be able to smell them all.

So, make sure the associations to all those smells are positive, happy, and calming.

To give you an example, when you see your dog about to go take a nap or rest, get one of the items you have washed with the future baby's detergent and go sit by your dog. Breathe in and out calmly and take your time. The dog might be a little excited to be next to you at first, perhaps. If that's the case, wait until he's calm, without saying anything. You can stroke him gently or leave him be (sometimes leaving your dog in peace, without touching him is better, so he can fully relax). When he's chilled and about to fall asleep or even already resting, just place the baby item on your lap and stay there for a bit. If you can't do it yourself, ask someone else to do it for you. If you are in a hurry, because you have got stuff to do, avoid the exercise all together. You need to be calm, not stressed out.

Try not to leave the baby item with the dog and then leave, unless you can still actively supervise the situation. Make sure that when your dog wakes up, he doesn't start playing with that item and wreck it. That baby item represents your baby. You wouldn't put your baby in the dog's bed, would you? And you wouldn't leave your baby next to the sleeping dog and leave the room or the house, would you? No, as these situations are a huge safety risk to your baby's health! Keep this in mind: when your dog is around the baby item, he ought to be calm and relaxed.

At other times, away from the baby items, play with your dog, have fun and allow him to run and let the crazy out; but as soon as the baby items reappear, go back to being calm, relaxed and away from too much doggy-silliness.

A note about crates:

Often, when I visit a family who is adopting a dog or about to have a baby, they show me they have already bought a crate, which I used to recommend a few years back. However, I have since changed my views due to increasing knowledge about dogs, but also working more with kids.

We need to give the dog a space to go away from the kids, where the dog can relax without being disturbed, but also where he can be kept safe from the children in the household or visiting kids, especially when active supervision isn't possible. Crates aren't ideal, simply because they can too easily be abused and turn into a cage or a prison, from where the child can tease the dog, even involuntarily. Even worse, the child sits in the crate with the dog, as if they were sharing a bedroom.

Such situations, I am sure, you've seen from

photos and videos on social media.

People tend to think that this looks cute or that it is sweet that the child wants to cuddle up with the dog in the crate. But it is neither cute, nor sweet. In fact, sadly, it is very invasive for the dog, which can lead them to feel increased stress or fear towards the child. Those feelings might be repressed for a long time, in some dogs certainly longer than others, but we all have a breaking point. I know I do, don't you?

When I reach my breaking point, I turn into a banshee, and I get the Medusa look too! Trust me, it's not a pretty sight! But I still have some control over my emotions, and I have never gotten to a point of full-on crazy, unless you consider when I was little and my brother and I used to fight, because back then I had little-to-no impulse control.

Before a dog reaches his breaking point, he would have given us plenty of body language signals to let us know. For dogs, biting is the last resort, yet if a dog keeps getting pushed and pushed and pushed, they will break, like all of us!

If he doesn't feel safe in the crate because the kids stand around pestering the dog, who is trapped and has nowhere to go, well, the poor dog has no other options but to defend himself and react negatively towards whoever is causing him that much stress. In this case, it would be the child.

By having a playpen, or a spare room, the dog

has much more space to navigate, giving him a way out of a situation that makes him feel uncomfortable.

Escape routes and having the choice to leave are so important to dogs and, when you think about it, they are important to us as well.

Chapter 7:

Newborn Around Dogs

A few days before our baby was born, my mother and my former sister-in-law, Lisa, came to stay with us to help with the first few days post-partum and because my mother was desperate to become a nonna (the Italian word for 'grandmother').

Having them around was lovely, and Pixel adored the attention and the extra food my mother kept giving him.

I will save you the drama of childbirth, but I will tell you this… they don't call it labour for nothing! I was in labour for 21 hours of atrocious pain and I thought multiple times that I was going to die.

However, I knew I would have something amazing at the end of all that excruciating amount of pain… and amazing she was. Our little Molly was born on May 28th 2011.

During my labour and the 2 days I had to stay in hospital after the delivery, Gary stayed with me as much as he could.

My parents-in-law came down from London, and with my mother and Lisa, they visited as much as the hospital allowed - at the time no more than 3 visitors were allowed in the room.

Pixel could have stayed with them at the flat, as he wouldn't have been left for too long, however we asked our neighbour, Lindsey, to look after him for us while I was in hospital.

We made that decision not only because Lindsey offered to have him, but because Pixel knew her, knew her house, loved her and her family, and he absolutely adored her Saint Bernard Muffyn. They were the best of friends, so I knew he would be in safe hands and happy there.

After my long labour, I was physically and mentally exhausted; yet I was stressed about how to hold, feed, change and ultimately perfectly care for my newborn, and not having to worry about Pixel was a massive help.

So, even after all these years, even if we are no longer in touch like we used to be and the gorgeous Muffyn has left this Earth, I can't tell you how grateful I am to Lindsey and her family for that time.

Caring for a newborn really does take a village, and this is my biggest advice to you. Don't be afraid to ask or accept help from others. I am saying this as someone who has always struggled with asking for help. But the little village made up of friends and family is there to help you and because they love you, so don't be afraid to reach out to them.

Sometimes, in your village, there might be professional help, like a dog walker, dog boarder, dog trainer or behaviourist.

And sometimes, there might be a need for extra help… especially after giving birth.

If you feel 'too unwell', if something isn't quite right, please reach out and ask for help from your doctor or someone you trust. Postpartum emotions feel like being on a rollercoaster and are very common, including postpartum depression. Please, know that you are not alone and that there are professionals out there that can help you with that.

When we got home, Pixel was already there with my mum and Lisa. Lindsey had brought him home, so he was there waiting for us.

Molly was in her car seat, which was detachable from the car, so Gary carried her in the car seat, and I followed. The very good thing about all that labour pain was that the PGP was gone almost instantly after delivering Molly and I could walk unaided again! I was never that happy to do some stairs in my life!

When we arrived at the flat Pixel was so excited! He hadn't seen me for almost 4 days, and we missed each other a lot.

Due to my stitches and just feeling a little 'delicate', I couldn't kneel well, so my mum took care of watching Molly while Gary and I cuddled our baby Pixel, now an older brother to his human sister.

Some books might tell you to greet your dog calmly when you come back with your baby, so the dog learns to be calm around you and, while that isn't wrong, I often thought it to be unrealistic, at least to me. I loved Pixel and he loved me, madly so! Displaying that love was part of our bond, so as along as Molly was safely strapped into her portable car seat, and not in the way of the cuddles we were having with Pixel. So, I didn't see why I had to change the way I greeted my beloved dog.

The funny thing was, before taking Molly home, our biggest worry that that Pixel would be all over Molly, but he wasn't. If anything, he seemed to ignore her.

It has been a few years, now, but I remember thinking that Pixel perhaps didn't care for her. I kept thinking 'What if he doesn't like her?' or 'What if they don't get on?'

Those were the rollercoaster of postpartum emotions in my head talking (again, completely normal), because now that I know a bit better, I believe that it was our preparation that helped him not to go completely nuts around her.

Still, we had to be careful. She was a little newborn baby, and he was a dog. No matter how much Gary and I loved him (and still do), no matter how we considered him to be our other child, we knew, we had to know, that he was still a dog. And for as sweet and lovely as he was, he did have the power to hurt his little baby sister.

This is why Pixel and Molly were never, ever allowed to be alone in a room, or to be with careless supervision.

Active supervision when Molly and Pixel were together was a priority, at all times.

My dad and my brother also came to stay a couple of days after I came back home from the hospital and Gary's family visited too. Our place had never been that busy!

While it was lovely to see everyone, it was also a bit overwhelming, and I felt that I didn't have much control over anything. Pixel was also a little overwhelmed, I am sure, as he couldn't have his usual 23-hour naps and, while he loved some of the attention, he was also seen by our visitors as 'something' to keep away from Molly at all times. For example, every time someone was visiting, and Pixel would go anywhere near Molly, mostly just to sit on someone's feet and rest, he would be moved away by our guests.

This was fully against what I and Gary believed and still believe. Molly and Pixel were going to be together, under the same roof and part of the same family for life. It would have been unreasonable and unfair to keep them apart forever.

What I wanted to create was a relationship between the two of them of mutual respect and affection. I wanted Pixel to be able to be curious and give Molly a sniff if he wanted, and either me or Gary (or another responsible adult) would have been there to prevent Pixel getting overexcited around Molly or, as Molly grew up, to prevent her from grabbing him or doing something to upset him.

However, as we all know, when dealing with your family members it is often very difficult to make your opinions heard. You don't want to upset anyone, and they always seem to know better, don't they?

For this very reason, having a professional coming to the house and even talking to the family is a brilliant idea! That is a third party, who has no blood-relation to you or the rest of the people there and who is qualified to talk about dogs and how to better handle dogs and kids together… or kids around dogs, if you will (see what I did there?).

Within a week, only my mum was left to help with Molly and Pixel. My dad, brother and Lisa had to go back to Switzerland to work and the flat felt much calmer again. It was nice having my mum around a little longer. She was doing all the cleaning and cooking, and I can't tell you how helpful that was!

However, after almost two weeks of her help, my mum had to leave too.

I was very sad to see my mum go. But I wasn't sad just because of all the help she gave us, which both Gary and I were so, so grateful for, but it was because Molly was, and still is, her only -human- granddaughter. My parents lived almost 2000 miles away and I know how much they wanted to be grandparents. I felt a lot of empathy towards my mother. Something that, perhaps, I couldn't feel quite as deeply before becoming a mother myself.

In a way, you could say, I felt sorry for her, and I felt guilty that my decisions were the reasons why we were so far away. However, I see it much more clearly now that those same decisions also lead us to create our beautiful, forever crying and never-sleeping baby. We had tried to get pregnant for so long when we lived in Switzerland, but just over a month back in the UK and we were successful. I think that really speaks volumes on how unhappy we were there and how things work out how they are meant to sometimes.

Still, I could be writing about all 'the law of attraction' in the world, but seeing my mother cry as she was telling us how she would miss us all, especially Molly, made me feel like my heart was breaking. It is a kind of pain I do not wish on anyone. And, for once, I didn't mind listening to her last recommendations, opinions and suggestions, which, believe me, were many!

When we came home after dropping her off at the airport, the flat felt so empty! It really was just the four of us and, soon enough, Gary went back to working his normal hours, even as a freelancer, so in a way, it was just Pixel, Molly, and me.

I felt like motherhood had really begun and it wasn't an easy ride.

Key points

I have learned to believe in the power of the expression 'it takes a village'. This is because accepting or even asking for help is at times essential.

Or maybe you have to hire someone, like a dog walker or house your dog at a dog boarder. Whatever options you have, make sure your dog has some time to adapt to the new environment and the new people who will look after him.

For example, if you are hiring a dog walker, make sure they get to meet you and your dog beforehand. I would suggest going on a walk together, perhaps.

If your dog goes to someone else's house, like a friend, family member or a dog boarder, give your dog time to get to know the person or people that will look after him. Ensure that you visit the house before his first day properly there and while you are still around, so he will feel safe in your presence.

This is particularly important with dog boarders, as you might not know them. Make sure they are licensed, as they must be legally in the UK. If they are licensed, it will give you that peace of mind that they will be insured, and that their premises are regularly checked by the council warden, who issues the license.

Leaving your dog with a dog boarder might not

be cheap, but they will look after the dog with a level of home-from-home care, or at least they ought to!

I advise you to go visit the dog boarding facility or house, chat to the boarders or staff and see who lives there. It's best if they come recommended by people you know and trust, but you also check reviews on social media, photos of the dogs that stay there and comments on posts online. Do your research, because you are leaving your precious furry child there, so you want to make sure he is happy and will be properly looked after.

Your dog and newborn

When you have a newborn, your house turns into a visitor's centre! It's unbelievable the number of people who want to come visit you and meet your baby. They will bring you love, gifts and many, many opinions, especially when it comes to the contact and interaction your dog should have with your baby.

They all mean well, I truly believe that, but they might not understand the level of love you have for your dog. They might not get that your dog is your other child and completely part of your family unit.

Whatever they suggest or if they want to share their opinions with you, I would say, just smile and thank them. Tell them you'll take their advice into consideration, that you will think about it and move on. There is no point in arguing too much about things. If they love you, they will also trust you will do the best you can by your baby and your dog and ideally should also trust your judgment.

I might not know you personally, but if you bought this book, I am sure it is because you want to do the best for your family, or kids around dogs, so I think you have pretty good judgment.

However, and I really speak from experience, some of the people in our life can be a little pushy and demanding when it comes to what they feel is right. If that is the case, why not have a **Kids Around Dogs®** professional come to your house and talk to you and your family about the best ways to help foster a good relationship between your baby and your dog?

After all, your dog and newborn will grow up together, share many adventures and make wonderful memories together. Hopefully those memories will include other people you love, so by having a professional around, talking to you and those people to show what you, your baby, and your dog really need to help everyone live in harmony.

Trust me, even the more insistent of friends or family members will feel reassured by knowing that you have called in the experts and that they have been invited to ask questions and to get some peace of mind.

Unwelcome opinions aside, visitors will be aplenty, especially during the first few days of your baby being born and at home, as hospital visits can be limited.

While it's beautiful to feel so much love from so many, it can also be tricky for your baby to have some time to relax and can be very stressful for your dog too!

I read somewhere that if all those visitors were to come to your place and do a little something to help you out, like letting you have a rest while they cuddle the baby; or clean a room in your house while they are there, then that would be the most helpful visit! Maybe having a suggestion box of things for visitors to help with would be a good idea!

I was lucky to have my mother around right after Molly was born, because she really did all the cooking and cleaning, and was extremely eager to hold Molly while she slept or helped her burping her after a feed.

When my mum left to go back to Switzerland, I truly realised how helpful she had been! Scrubbing the toilet while my baby was crying behind me wasn't as fun or as comical as it might sound! Especially when you consider that a baby crying made me produce more milk, instantly! Some days were just ridiculous, really!

Anyway, I am digressing, but what I wanted to point out was that all those people visiting might throw you off a little, might make your baby more tired than she needs to be and might stress your dog out, even if he loves the company and he's the friendliest of dogs.

When people tell you they want to visit, why not create a scheduled visiting time? Or, if it's someone you know very well and trust, why not be honest and ask for help? Remember, it takes a village!

Tell them that you need to do the laundry and take a shower and ask them if they would mind helping and looking after the baby while you look after yourself? If they're friends, they'll do it and they'll be happy to give you a helping hand. After all, they might be there to see you also, but they are mostly there to meet your baby, which they can do while you do other stuff.

Just remind them not to leave the dog and the baby unsupervised, or with passive supervision like them playing on their phone around the dog and baby. If you are worried about this, why not take your dog with you? If you need a shower, bring the dog into the bathroom with you. If you are doing the laundry, get him to follow you, or use a lead attached to you (to your belt, for example) to ensure that your dog is with you at all times.

I would like to make sure the topic of post-partum depression or similar mental health struggles are acknowledged here.

I am not a therapist, nor did I suffer from postpartum depression to its higher degrees, however I know from women who have experienced it it can be incredibly scary. Our hormones and minds can play weird tricks on us. Please, know that you are not alone. Know that there is help out there and do not be afraid to reach out. By getting the help you need to feel better, you will also be able to better care for your baby and your family.

If you, or a loved one are showing signs of postpartum depression, make sure to get in contact with a doctor, who will be able to guide you accordingly.

Don't wait and don't think it'll just go away because it might not. It might actually get worse, making you feel needlessly mentally and often physically unwell.

Finally, but this is possibly the most important point... forgive yourself! Remember, you are only human! It's hard to be a parent, especially of a newborn. So, prepare as much as you can in advance, manage the situations the best you can, plan ahead, ask for help (or seek it out), but at the end of the day, remember you are doing amazingly well!

Be proud of yourself!

Chapter 8:

Motherhood Around Dogs

Actively supervising interactions between Pixel and Molly was always a priority! The rule was that Pixel and Molly were never to be left alone together.

This meant that I was either in between Molly and Pixel, or holding Molly when Pixel was near me. Or, at the very least, I would be part of whatever interaction Pixel and Molly had.

If I could not guarantee to be alert, even if physically present, I would put Molly in her cot, Moses basket, baby-chair, or in her playpen.

We bought a baby rocker that we moved into various rooms when needed, like the bathroom, so that Molly could be in there safely, while I used the bathroom or showered. If I was busy doing something, I would close the door so that Pixel wouldn't just walk in when I couldn't give them both my full attention.

The stair gate in the kitchen guaranteed that I could have Molly in the same room in the rocker while I was cooking or doing the dishes or whatever, while Pixel would have the rest of the house to use. Often, while I fed Molly, she would be on that special nursing pillow that I was gifted. After a good feed, she would fall asleep on it and indirectly on me. When that happened, I could not move, or she would wake up. So, I spent many,

many, many hours in that position and Pixel would snuggle up next to me.

Gary was working and helped as much as he could, but he couldn't feed the baby (as I was breastfeeding) and our little Molly was one hungry baby! Molly didn't have set mealtimes as some babies seem to do. Moreover, we were suggested to feed when the baby needed it and she seemed to need it every 3 minutes, day or night.

I was tired. No, I was more than tired... I literally felt like I was drunk. Honestly, I had never felt like that before.

I would watch the sunrise and I would hear the gentle snoring of Gary coming from the bedroom. All I could think of was that I wanted to carve his eyes out. Why should he sleep and not me?

Ah! Don't worry, my husband is alive and well, but we did talk about how I was feeling. How tired I was, how I needed to sleep. So, we tried for a few nights to swap places. This could only work at the weekend, when he didn't have work the next day, but I would express as much breastmilk as I could, which really wasn't much, and Pixel and I went to sleep in the guest room on the sofa bed. (This room was to be Molly's room eventually). Gary would be in our bedroom, with Molly in the Moses basket next to him. We tried that set up and magically she did give me about 3 hours of sleep, so we decided to try again.

Pixel had always slept with us, and we never thought anything of it, so we carried on that way even after Molly was born. Funny how I imagined that I would instantly fall asleep that first night without Molly, but I didn't... I kept imagining Gary calling me, or I would hear Molly crying, or I would worry because she wasn't crying and then, of course, I would feel like I should be cleaning or tidying up the house. Now that I had 'some me time'... as if sleeping was secondary to tidying up the place.

Seriously, what was wrong with me? Even as I type this, remembering it all, I can't help feeling like I really want to scream at my old-self to just 'Go To Sleep!!'.

The little experiment of Pixel and me sleeping in a separate room for one night a week didn't last too long, as Molly wouldn't settle with the expressed milk in a bottle and it gave her the worst colic. So, that one night was that.

Not only Molly wouldn't sleep at night, but the day-time was also a challenge. I remember I would take her for drives during the day, to help her sleep. She liked that and it always worked a treat. I remember sitting in car parks by the beach in Bournemouth or Sandbanks and looking at the sea, with Molly sleeping in the car seat. If I dared to move her, she would wake up and I would have to drive around some more. I am almost ashamed to admit that I did 'rest my eyes' a couple of times in the car while parked somewhere.

Obviously, I knew there were many problems with that... firstly, was that I should not have been driving feeling so tired! I had months of sleep-deprivation, and my concentration was affected by that. I knew that a car seat wasn't designed as a substitute for a baby cot, so she shouldn't have been sleeping in there for too long. Also, she was getting used to sleeping in the car and not at home. But she wouldn't sleep at home... it was all a vicious cycle, and I was in the middle of it all.

Gary and I read up so much about the topic of why babies don't sleep. We watched videos of experts in the field, listened to and tried all the advice people were giving. Nothing worked! All Molly wanted was breast milk and me... the two came together, but because I was so tired, the breast milk was also lacking. So, in utter desperation I called the midwife and cried while on the phone with her. There was a phone helpline for these kinds of things and after the call with the midwife they called me back that very day. I explained what was happening with Molly and that we were just so desperate, as we didn't know what to do.

The lady told us to let her cry it out.

This woman, whose name I can't remember, told us to let her cry, alone in her cot, and she'll be fine.

And so, as a very desperate new mum, I did what I was told- this was a person in authority after all, she knew what was right. So, I sat on the floor, outside Molly's door, listening to her cry, bawling my eyes out. Pixel was by my side, probably wondering why I wasn't going to take care of the screaming baby. This did not sit well with me, but I was exhausted. I know Gary didn't like it either, but we didn't know what else to do.

She was 8 months old by then. I had probably slept a total of 10 hours combined in 8 months- ok, probably a little more, but not that much more. I knew I couldn't take it anymore, so I had no choice but to sit there, crying and waiting for her to stop. The first night she cried for a solid hour. We had a monitor, we knew she was safe, but at the consultant's instructions, we didn't go in.

It took Molly a week of us doing that for her not to cry. I finally did get my night sleep and many nights after that, but I regret now what I did then. I regret listening to that advice, because I am sure that some of the fears and anxieties Molly had and still experiences is because of us letting her cry it out, instead of making her feel safe and secure.

If I could go back in time, I would have asked for help. I would have reached out to my neighbour Lindsey and our family more. But I didn't. I thought that I would have looked incapable of looking after my own child if I had. During these challenging months, Lindsay, who had helped with Pixel before, helped me twice by dog sitting Pixel. The only reason I let her is because she offered without really taking 'no' for an answer. One time was when she saw how tired I looked and another time was when Gary and I got sick, so she came to help us out, bravely not even worrying about catching what we had.

People do tell you that it's hard to have a baby, and I don't mean to scare anyone with what I wrote, but I feel that the world behind the first few months of parenthood isn't talked about enough. It is harder than hard and no matter how much love that you have in your heart for your partner and your baby, at some point, you will resent them both.

Funnily enough, I never resented Pixel. But I often did think 'oh, now I have to look after you as well', as if he was yet another chore, rather than the boy who I loved and adored. Even now, after all this time, remembering those thoughts makes me feel so guilty.

So, how did we handle life for Pixel with a baby and no sleep?

Well, I could finally walk again unlike during my pregnancy, so we did resume strolls together with the pram. We showed Pixel the pram as soon as we bought it, and he was familiar with it. We had trained him to walk nicely-ish on the lead and we had combined the two. The only thing we didn't think of was that when you are so beyond tired, your body is also a little bit weaker. Also, you are pushing your real-life baby, and that baby is your first, so there is a sense of extra worry involved that isn't there when you just practice pre-baby. But Pixel was awesome and did very well. There had been a few regrettable side-pulls where I thought the pram would fall to the side, baby and all, but that never happened. If I could go back, I would certainly work on walking nicely on the lead by the pram more. Much, much more.

I don't know what dog you have or how many dogs you have but using positive reinforcement training for a good loose lead walking becomes even more important when you have a pram or pushchair to add to the equation.

Key Points

When it comes to dogs and kids of all ages, the very first thing to consider and to always keep in mind is that they need **active supervision** whenever they are together. It doesn't matter how old the dog is, what breed he is, how good he is and that you've known him forever and he would never hurt a fly; a dog is a dog. While dogs are incredibly loving creatures, they have the physical power to hurt us, and especially babies and young children who are more delicate and vulnerable. Therefore, we need to pay extra attention to dogs around kids.

Similarly, children, especially little ones, can be a little crazy sometimes. They are a bundle of cuteness, of course, but their minds and bodies are still developing, so often they do things we wouldn't dream of, simply because they are learning how to live in the world. Such as what is good and what is bad, how things operate and more. Young children don't understand danger, they often just see opportunities, adventures, they need to satisfy their curiosity. And, while some children will be calmer and less inquisitive than others, all children, at some point, will act in ways that we as adults don't expect or even understand.

So, when you see a child pulling a dog's tail, that is not the child being 'naughty' or 'disrespectful', that is a child seeing something fluffy and interesting and wanting to know what it does. It is likely that her very young, growing brain, sends messages like 'What happens if you pull it? Let's find out' and the body acts accordingly. Moreover, often they see people around them freaking out if they do something they shouldn't, making that action even more interesting. So, it is likely that their brain will go 'Did you see mum running up to me when I pulled the fluffy thing? That was interesting, let's see if she does it again!'.

By being a proactive parent and an active supervision parent, you can avoid all that troublesome thinking all together or preventing your child's impulse from hurting your dog. Thereby, keeping kids and dogs safe and happy.

You might be wondering what active supervision is. And if there is passive supervision. Indeed, there is! Let me explain it all properly:

Active supervision is the only supervision you should apply when kids and dogs are together. It is the kind of supervision that needs you to be both physically and mentally present. You should either be between the kids and dogs, help them with the interaction, or watch them at a close distance. If you are on your phone, you are not actively supervising. If you are cooking, you are not actively supervising. If you are reading a book, even if it is THIS book, you are not actively supervising. You might be in the same room as your kids and your dogs, but you are busy doing something else, so how can you concentrate on your child, your dog, and your favourite TV show?

Passive supervision is when you are in the same

room as your kids and your dogs, but you are distracted. You might be 'resting your eyes', tidying up the room, making yourself a cup of tea, or sending an email or text message, or doing a little of work. Whatever it is that you are doing in that space and time, if you are not actively participating in the activities that your dogs and your kids are doing, you are only there passively. This can lead to problems.

I would also urge you to be a proactive parent, not a reactive one. By this I mean to think ahead, so that we always set up our dogs and our kids for a positive, good, and safe interaction. For example, if your child is keen on playing with the dog, why not buy a long tug toy, or a flirt pole? That way your child, with your help, can hold one end of the tug toy, while the dog plays with the other end, with a safe distance away from little hands.

Another example of being proactive is to anticipate how your dog might react to something that your child might do. For example, say your little one has a rocker with music and toys all around it. And, every time the baby is in there, the dog gets very excited, jumps about, and tries to get on the rocker with the baby, or tries to get one of the toys. Having the dog get to that level of excitement isn't good for anyone, dog included, so it is best to have the dog in a different location, like another room, before placing the baby in her rocker.

Similarly, if you know your toddler gets super excited when the dog is resting in his bed, because he looks 'soooo cute' when he's asleep- then have your dog sleep or rest in a separate room or in a playpen that your child has no access to. If the kids are at the age where they can walk and start working out how to open doors, it is best to have the dog locked in a room, so the children can't open it when you can't actively supervise their interaction.

If the dogs and kids are together and their interaction isn't a good one, you have to intervene, that's reactive parenting. While this is still better than passive supervision, it is still a risky one, as your reaction might come too late, or it might have a negative effect on the relationship that your dog and child are creating.

So, think and plan ahead, and be there mind, body and soul!

Here is a beautiful infographic by my colleague and friend Jennifer Dawson Shryock, founder of Family Paws to help you further understand the concept of supervision of kids and dogs:

The training side of things is super important for all dogs, but I would say, especially when there are kids of all ages in the household.

<u>When a baby or toddler is around, you need to have certain behaviours in place, such as:</u>

Walking nicely on the lead

Because you will have your pushchair or pram, you need to make sure the dog won't pull you and your baby over as you walk.

A solid recall

Your dog needs to be safe at all times, and shouldn't disturb other people or animals, so you need to be able to have him back when needed. Moreover, there will be a time when your baby starts screaming because she's been sick or done the 1000th poo of the day. Or you forgot or ran out of nappies or wipes, and you can't change her in the middle of the park, so you have to turn around and go back home. If your dog doesn't come back when called, you'll have a screaming baby, a runaway dog and your stress levels will be insane.

The cues 'sit' or 'down'

Between these two cues, I prefer the dog to lay down. This is especially important for big dogs, as even in a sitting position they can reach a child's head. Either cue can be used to prevent the dog from jumping up at the kids. Additionally, it is a position associated with relaxation (if you have helped the dog to make that association) and it is also seen as polite behaviour for society, which, as we know, can be so very judgmental, especially when a dog lives with kids.

Leave

Dogs like to pick stuff up all the time, whether the items belong to them or not, it doesn't matter to dogs. However, they might pick up something that belongs to the child, something expensive, something precious, or something dangerous. Whatever it is, unless it is theirs and they can have it at that time, teaching them to 'leave' something can make a huge difference in a household with kids. Especially as you'll notice how much more stuff you'll suddenly have when there's a child in the house and how much less time you can dedicate to keeping it all tidy.

Give or drop

Sometimes we get to the dogs too late, and they have already gotten the items they aren't allowed to have. Teaching them a solid 'give' or 'drop' will be lifesaving! You really don't want the dog to start stealing the baby's toys, bottles, or whatever else.

If, the dog gets something that doesn't belong to him, please, no matter how stressed you are- try to stay calm. If you get worked up, or start chasing the dog, or, if in any way you react too much in that moment, it might turn 'stealing' into a game, which will encourage the dog more. If you start chasing or yelling at your dog when they have something that doesn't belong to them, this might make the dog think that he ought to protect what he takes. He may even start reacting negatively towards people that come close to him when he has a new or known item in his mouth or has any form of physical contact with the item.

This is a form of what is called resource guarding, a behaviour where dogs feel they need to protect what they perceive as a valuable resource, such as a toy that they love very much. When a dog that resource guards sees someone approaching while he is interacting with an item that he loves, he might worry that it will be taken away from him. So, he will find ways to protect it, like sitting on it, walking away with it, snarling, or growling or more. Teaching a solid 'give' or 'drop' can help prevent many of these issues.

Peekaboo

This behaviour is also called 'middle', is when the dog walks behind you and appears between your legs, where he will stay. This can be super helpful when children and other dogs are around, as long as you make sure others don't touch your dog when he is in a 'peekaboo'. That way, the dog will know that in this position, he is safe. Nobody, **kids included**, can annoy him or disturb him. Moreover, it is a great trick to prevent the dog from jumping up at people, as he'll be between your legs, and not jumping up at the group of kids playing football. It is also an incredibly cute behaviour!

Especially when you have a new baby at home, your dog should be able to be left and sleep alone. He should ideally not sleep in the parents' bed or bedroom and certainly not in the baby nursery.

There will be times when you need to go to the doctor, or activities like Mommy and Me classes, or when you simply can't actively supervise your dogs and kids, so the dog will have to be left alone, without you or anyone, for a certain amount of time. If your dog gets stressed or anxious when you or anyone else leave, this can be extremely stressful and detrimental to the health and welfare of the dog. It can also be incredibly difficult for you to manage life with a baby. However, in the majority of cases, this can be helped, but it does take some time, so start as soon as you can.

As you have probably gathered, I have nothing against sleeping with dogs! I loved it when Pixel slept with us! He was super gentle, and his methodical snoring was very calming for me. He was also a snuggler, and I always enjoyed our cuddles. However, when our daughter arrived, having Pixel in our bed did make things more complicated and I wished I had worked on him sleeping somewhere else, so that stress could have been avoided too.

It is a matter of safety. When you are sleeping, you are not actively supervising, so it's as if you are not even in the room. If the dog is on your bed and your baby or young child gets up, who's to say that she won't startle the dog, which might cause him to negatively react? Even if your baby is waking up and crying in the middle of the night, you might be too tired to pay full attention to your dog, while going to check on the baby and maybe even taking the baby to your bed. I know you love your dog and I know you might think your dog would never hurt your baby, but is it worth finding out? Is it really worth the risk?

If you need help in any of these areas, check out

our Kids Around Dogs® professional directory!

Always look for a force-free dog trainer, so you and your dog will be working without anything upsetting going on. No pain, no shouting, no telling off! There is no need for any of that! Remember, concentrate on management first, so have stairgates, playpens, spare room available.

Work with your dog so that he is ok with being left in his 'dog nook' even before the baby arrives. If you know that you are going to have some particularly challenging days ahead or if you feel you need support, reach out to friends, family, or professionals (like a registered/licenced daycare or dog boarder).

Lastly, I want to say something about expectations versus reality. My daughter was born in a social media society. Facebook was already well-known and so was Twitter. Instagram was just starting out, so not much used yet. At the time I was part of some parenting Facebook groups and other blogs and forums, where I would read about other parents and how they were coping at this thing. I swear, reading those articles or posts was only making me feel worse! Everyone else seemed to have the perfect baby, who always slept and pooped on command. The whole world had the perfect family, super clean house, a saint of a dog. The whole world, but me! I would look around and my house was a mess! And there was way too much dog fur (pugs shed like mad!). And, while Pixel was perfect in so many ways, he had never slept away from us, so he didn't like it when we tried that ONE time; and wasn't great on the lead (luckily, he was a small dog, so not too bad, but we should have worked on that).

I often felt terrible, inadequate and not a good mum. I still feel like that at times, but I am also learning to let go of stuff more and I am learning, more and more, that you shouldn't believe everything people post on social media.

I too tend to post only the good times, like visiting Santa at Christmas, or fabulous photos from a fancy holiday, or a new haircut. You aren't going to see that Molly cried the first time she met Santa or that those fabulous holiday photos are followed by an upset child or my horrible sunburn because I forgot to put suntan lotion on myself, while the kid is plastered in it. And my new haircut? Often, it's because I'm so insecure about it that I want others to tell me it looks good, as I don't believe the hairdresser!

This is to say, be kind to yourself. You are doing an amazing job as a parent of kids and dogs! You are, in fact, doing an amazing job at life! And, hey, if you are reading this book, it means you have very good literary judgment too!

Chapter 9:

Toddlers Around Dogs

As Molly kept growing, I started to do more baby-related activities. I was very keen to make some mum-friends and for Molly to do stuff that excited her. I was also very interested to see what she enjoyed doing and to give her a chance to experience fun stuff in life.

We went to Baby Sensory ™, Sing and Sign, Baby & Mummy dance, swimming lessons, Baby & Mummy yoga, Baby & Mummy walks and stretch (or some name like that), and many of the gatherings that the local children centres were offering. Although all the mums were lovely and friendly, I didn't seem to 'click' with anyone, until I met Grainne and her son Max.

Max is almost 4 months older than Molly, who was just 6 months old when we met. He was a super cute and super good boy! Every time we'd see each other, he was either napping or calmly sitting in his pushchair. I was envious of how calm that baby was, compared to my little hurricane girl. Molly didn't like the pushchair and always wanted to get out of there and be either with me or on the floor, which was unhygienic when out and about and impossible to manage.

So, I approached Max's mum and asked her how she did it. I know it sounds like a mental thing to do, but at that point I hadn't slept for about 6 months... all my sanity was gone! She smiled modestly and said something like "Oh, he's not always like this". And that's how I knew I liked her. You have no idea of how many mums would have replied, "Thank you, I am so lucky! My baby sleeps all the time, I'm so perfect and you are not!"- or something of the sort. We exchanged numbers and agreed to meet up for a walk the following week.

On that occasion, I left Pixel home. I had only just met Grainne and Max and I didn't know how Max would be around dogs. I wanted to be able to concentrate on Molly and to get to know our new acquaintances. Did I feel bad about leaving Pixel home? Of course, I did! He would have been there for sure, in our life before Molly. But, when a small human joins the family, some changes have to be made. Leaving him home when meeting other children for the first time was one of those changes. It was the sensible thing to do, and it gave the kids a chance to have fun.

The first time Molly and I went out with Grainne and Max was at a local park, with a lovely playground in it. I hadn't really taken Molly to a playground yet as I didn't think she could go on anything. But Grainne had two older girls, Maya and Eva, so she had that confidence and knowledge that I, a first-time mother, was lacking. When she put Max in a baby-swing (which has a layer of protection around the body of the baby), I held my breath, thinking that was not going to work... but it did. So, I felt brave enough for Molly to have a go too. My little girl was hooked!! I had never seen her that happy! Her face had the biggest smile, and her little legs were kicking, and it was a truly beautiful, yet so simple moment!

That day, not only did I learn to trust my baby a little more, but I also learned that Grainne was a jewellery maker and, at the time, was also offering casting of baby hands and feet, which of course, I had to have! Little did I know that I had just had my first meet up with the woman who would become my best friend and that her son, Max, would be almost like a brother to Molly, even today.

Grainne and Max became a big part of Molly and my life, as we got together more often and we trusted each other with our little ones too, which I feel is extremely important. Grainne knew of my struggles and suggested that we helped each other out. She wanted to have more time to build her business, *Times to Treasure*, while I needed more time to regain my sanity, so agreed for Grainne to look after both Max and Molly one morning a week, and I would do the same another morning of the week. Our plan worked out amazingly well for the kids and both of us. Soon enough, the morning became a whole day and sometimes, even more than once a week. If one of us needed help, the other one was there.

Gary was very happy about this plan, as he was feeling guilty about not being able to help me as much and, I think, Grainne's partner Pep was also happy about it, as he was also working and couldn't be there all the time for Grainne. As I mentioned before, Max had two older sisters, Maya and Eva, who were of school age and had, at the time, a bit more independence, but still needed their mum. So, sometimes, Grainne would be with them while Max was with me and, other times, Molly would spend time with them all.

I wonder how Molly felt about going from a house where she was the only child to a fuller house, with other 3 kids around. I know she loved them all and, for a while at least, they were like a second family to her, which I was very happy about. To me, friends can be a family that you find for yourself. I knew, and still know today, how lucky I am to have met Grainne and to have her and her family in our life.

How did Pixel fit into all of this? Well, he fitted in pretty well!

Max didn't have any pets, apart from a lovely bunny called Jojo, who lived in an enclosure in their garden. His older sister, Maya, was allergic to animals, which is something that would upset her very much. In fact, both Eva and Maya are very clever, caring and animal lover girls, which made Maya's allergy very difficult to accept.

When Max met Pixel for the first time it was during a walk on the beach. I told them that I would bring our doggy, but I am not sure this information registered with Max, as he was only about 11 months old then. Pixel was happy to be at the beach and a little excited when I got him out of the car. I should have given him more time to have good sniffs around and get some of that energy out before meeting with new people, especially a little child. But I did keep Pixel on the lead and Max was sitting in his pushchair when we saw each other. Pixel was used to pushchairs because of Molly's, so he was ok with that. His little tail was going so fast, and his bottom was wiggling with it too- it was like a wiggle machine. Grainne gave him lots of lovely cuddles, while Max just kind of stared at him for a while, which I understand, and think was very sensible. Now that I know Max and have worked with many children, I understand that Max was simply working out what the situation was. It was a new event, he wasn't used to dogs, pugs also look very different from 'normal' dogs. Additionally, he wasn't expecting this to happen (even if previously told) and he couldn't comprehensively understand it yet, so his brain was trying to make sense of it all. Reaching for something familiar, something he could recognise, that could make him understand and that could make sense to him. Grainne told him that the doggy was Pixel and he was Molly's doggy.

Molly was in her pushchair, munching on a baby biscuit, happy as she could be.

Was she aware that her new friend was working hard to connect with the situation? Was she aware that Pixel was excited, but also starting to calm down as we were too and weren't doing anything to keep his excitement going?

I honestly doubt it.

Pixel was a big part of our life and our family. So, I wanted to make sure Max got to know him, and Pixel got to know Max in a positive, friendly and calming way.

A walk by the beach, in a neutral place, and with things to distract both Max and Pixel, seemed like the best place and it was. We had a lovely walk, cold but nice, and Max had plenty of opportunities to look at Pixel and for both of them to get used to each other.

Pixel also could observe Max, had the choice to walk near his pushchair if he wanted, and just having a good time with this new little human around.

Max and Pixel met a few more times outside on walks like the one at the beach, to get to know each other more and, during that time, Max started to walk. This was an amazing milestone in his life, and I couldn't wait for Molly to be on her feet too. Babies can start walking from the age of 9 months. Max was about 10 months old when he started walking, so he was considered an early walker.

What a lovely thing to see! This wobbly little boy taking a few steps, stopping, walking some more, being a bit wobbly, taking a few more steps and then sitting on the floor, probably tired from this new 'thing' that he could do.

Watching him walk was funny, cute, and incredibly fascinating, too. Obviously, my mind went to Pixel and how he would take those new movements, along with the worry that walking babies are at a delicate stage of their life. Their walk is unstable, their mind is still deciding what to do with their body and how to move it properly. Any dog could knock them over easily.

That concerned me a bit, so I made sure Pixel was always on the lead while Max was practising his new-found walking skills. I also made sure Molly watched him, so that she could learn from him. Mostly, however, she was busy eating something or wanting to be picked up.

We finally invited Max and Grainne over to our place, so that Pixel could get used to Max at our flat, since Grainne and I had agreed to start helping each other out, which meant Max would soon be spending time at our place and I wanted to make sure everything was going to be ok. Pixel, of course, wasn't the only reason we invited them over. Max hadn't been to our place yet, and it was important he got to see it and meet Gary while his mum was there, to help him feel comfortable and reassured if he needed it during the visit.

Luckily, I seem to remember that Max wasn't fazed by being somewhere new, meeting my husband or having Pixel around.

We approached things nicely, but without worrying too much either. Dogs are great at sensing when something is wrong, different, or 'off' somehow. So I didn't want to make it too much of a big deal, while knowing that, of course, that it was. When Grainne arrived, she was holding Max, and we let Pixel sniff Max's feet. We didn't ask Pixel to go check out Max, we didn't push either child or dog to do anything. Max was safe with his mum. Pixel was happy, inquisitive, but well behaved in expressing that joy and curiosity. He did his sniffing, some spinning of excitement, wagged his tail and bottom and happily accepted Grainne petting him with one hand, while holding Max with the other.

Pixel's preference was always me or Gary, so after some novelty excitement, he would check in with me and, if asked, he would come to me. When I went to the kitchen to get something to drink, Pixel followed me (and Molly), rather than staying with Grainne and Max.

Molly started walking about 2 weeks after turning 1. And, while I think I had spent every single second with her, I missed that special moment. Gary was with her and told me that she stood up, which she had done before, then took her first couple of steps towards Pixel and finally sat on the floor near him. All of this was completely supervised, with my husband right behind her and then he picked her up to come tell me what had just happened. I was in the kitchen cooking, and to this day, I'm absolutely gutted I missed it.

Looking after Max, even if only once a week or so, was a big help for Pixel to incrementally adjust to a small human to walking around him all the time, so he didn't seem that bothered when she started that phase of her life. His reactions were mostly related to what we as the parents were doing such as being excited for Molly's first few steps, or words, or any other new thing.

When Molly started walking, I was worried, excited, curious…. At once all emotions flooded through me, which Pixel could pick up on and was therefore more alert. It was as if he was saying: 'There's something I need to pay attention to'. By being calmer ourselves, even in those so-very important milestones in your baby's life, you can help your dog to feel calm too.

Key Points

It is essential to prepare your dog to be without you before the baby comes and to carry on building on that after your baby joins the family.

If your dog has any difficulty coping when you leave or separation anxiety issues, it is even more important to start helping him or her out as soon as possible. As such behaviour modification can take a very long time to be help your dog be able to cope for a life with kids around. Moreover, these behavioural concerns are not to be taken lightly and should be addressed with the help of a qualified professional.

A child's brain is in constant development and does an enormous job gathering information, retaining information, creating new solutions to new problems, and more! All this, while growing the body of a tiny little human. So, it is highly unlikely that Molly's brain would have also had the time or space to worry about her friend Max or her furry brother Pixel.

This is yet another reason why an adult's active supervision is essential for their safety.

Your attention, as a fully grown person, with a fully developed brain, has to always be focused on the kids and dogs, when they are together. If you are on the phone, you are not paying attention. If you are watching the waves at the beach, you are not paying attention. If you are watching tv, cooking, reading a book, you are not paying attention.

I think there are two crucial moments when kids and dogs meet at the dog's house.

One is at the beginning when the dog might be overly excited to have someone over. The dog might jump up, wag his tail a lot (which might be an issue with dogs with big tails), some dogs might even bark when overexcited. In that case, it is good to know what your dog does when someone comes over to visit, and work on preventing behaviours that may upset or even hurt a child. The other is to keep the dog on a lead, at least at first, to prevent some unwanted behaviour, and to make sure you 'have the dog', should the child or/and parent have some concerns too.

The second is when the children have been there for a little while. Typically, at first kids can be a bit reserved, even shy when they enter a home for the first time. However, once they are comfortable in a situation, new place or people, they get more talkative, they move around more, they start touching things and that includes getting more confident with the dog. This often happens when the dog has calmed down and, perhaps, decides to take a nap or to just chill around the humans.

Effectively, this is where the two species (child and dog) clash. One gets more active (the child), the other more chilled (the dog). This is also when most grownups are busy chatting with their visitors, or 'forgot' their dog was there, simply because the dog is resting and not bothering anyone. The adults might take a step back from being vigilant and from actively supervising, which can lead to problems. Such as the child approaching the dog when he shouldn't; or the dog getting excited again because the child is more active and, therefore, presenting behaviours that might be dangerous for a small child, even if the dog does them innocently and playfully.

For example, the tail of a beautiful and happy Vizla can feel like a whip when quickly wagging. Or a sweet, goofy Golden Retriever can easily knock over wobbly toddlers just by walking past them. Trust me, toddlers fall down like little bowling pins! And for as fun as that might sound, they can get hurt and they can even start building a fear of dogs.

Please, know that I am not saying small children and dogs shouldn't be together, because not only that would be impossible, but I also firmly believe that kids and dogs can make each other's life a better one! However, we need to actively supervise when kids and dogs are together. We need to be alert and be there, mind and body fully present.

If we can't properly supervise, then use management in your home to separate your dog and children. Such as stair gates, playpens, spare rooms- there are so many alternatives that can keep dogs and kids safe. Nowadays all those things come in all sorts of designs, so they can be rather pretty yet functional in any home.

When toddlers are about and walking, we also need to be considering that they fall over a lot! They are still learning how to walk properly, learning how to coordinate their body, and making all the right connections. When they fall over, they will likely look around for something to hold onto so they can get up again. This could be a piece of furniture, your hand, or the dog. They want to hold onto whatever they can because this is all they can concentrate on at that moment. Their need and want to get up is their entire focus and nothing else matters. Their brain is still developing, so it is too busy ensuring that the toddler is surviving. and helping their body grow, to comprehend the potential dangers about the dog the child is using as a 'lifter'.

However, that simple action from a toddler using the dog to get up can be distressing and even painful for the dog. What if the child gets hold of one of the dog's ears, grabs it tightly as they get up. Then that child's brain understands that ears will hold the toddler's entire body weight. So, the child tightly holds onto the dog's ear and gets up. Probably, then the toddler would then let go of the dog's ear and off they go walking.... Until the next time they fall.

Innocent enough, right? Mmm... not really! During that time the dog had to endure a certain amount of pain, an invasion of space, a lack of consent in being touched in a delicate area. That is a lot to ask of anyone, let alone an animal.

By actively supervising, you can immediately notice when your child has fallen or needs something to hold on to. So, you can offer your hand or point to the closest piece of furniture for your toddler to hold onto, like the edge of the sofa, a chair, a coffee table... anything, but the dog.

If you think those might seem details, think again. Your toddler will be playing the 'falling down' game like a million times a day! So, you will need to know how to handle such situations.

Please, remember that if you feel tired or this game has been going on all day, then you can arrange the toddler in a playpen and let your dog be free to roam the house (or vice versa).

Chapter 10:

Pre-schoolers Around Dogs

By the time Molly was 3 years old, the arrangement Grainne and I had helping each other out was going really well and the kids were happily spending whole days together. It was great!

However, Max was going to start pre-school, and I needed to start working properly. At the time, I had a little online job as a translator for an Italian website and I had one adult student to whom I was teaching Italian privately at my place, with Molly there. Unfortunately, then and now, one salary (my husband's) simply wasn't enough to sustain a family.

It was my choice to move to another country, away from my mum and dad. I never regretted my choice, but I often wished I could have called on my mum for some free childcare, like I saw so many other mothers around me doing.

I tried to get Molly into the same pre-school as Max, which was a very beautiful nursery in the middle of a place called Compton Acres. It is a stunning location surrounded by ornamental gardens. Daily, the children there would have little walks in the safety and beauty of the gardens. By doing this, the children were prepared to start their day at school with love and care. Oh, how badly I wanted Molly to go there! However, the waiting list was incredibly long, and we had very little chance.

Finally, I managed to find a lovely nursery in Poole, which seemed caring and fun and whose owner could speak some Italian. I hoped the owner could help Molly learn my mother tongue, as I was failing at that rather miserably. Although I taught others Italian, it never came naturally to me to speak Italian to my daughter- I don't know why. We had decided to place Molly at nursery in Poole rather than Bournemouth because we were house-hunting there and ready to move as soon as the right house would 'magically' appear to us. House-hunting wasn't as easy or as fun as we had imagined.

Both Gary and I had a dream of giving Pixel a garden. We had only lived in apartments with him, and I hope he had never wanted for anything. But we had always imagined Pixel wishing to pop out safely to get some fresh air whenever he wanted. We really wished to give that to him.

Luckily, Molly starting nursery wasn't an enormous change for Pixel. This was definitely due to the fact that Molly had been spending time away at Grainne's house, so our doggy was used to some time without her. That arrangement, from Pixel's side of things, had been very helpful.

Because we needed to get the children gradually used to being away from their respective mothers and homes, our plan had indirectly and accidentally given time to Pixel to easily adapt to that change, too. I say accidentally, because at the time, I honestly I didn't think about how the child suddenly 'disappearing' for a whole day while at nursery would be a big change for the dog too.

When you reach this milestone with your child, be sure to keep an eye on your dog. I am not saying you need to give them extra love, although you might inevitably do so at the beginning. Because, at least in my case, that first day at nursery I cried in the car after I left Molly at daycare. It was my first time leaving her somewhere that wasn't Grainne's house and while it needed to happen, it also hurt me doing it.

Thankfully that first day was only half-day. After I left Molly and collected myself, I came back home and took Pixel for a walk at the park. Just the two of us, like so many times before Molly was born. It wasn't a day of house-hunting, job-seeking, or soul-searching. It was a day to look after the upset mum in me, a day to remind myself there are other things I enjoy and want to do and it is ok for me to do them, even if I was/am a mum. It was a day where I had to remind myself that I was someone other than Molly's mum.

Remembering who I was before I was a mum was a very difficult thing indeed.

Before I knew it, it was time to go pick Molly up. When I arrived, that hug with her never felt warmer or sweeter. However, she was also tired and slightly in a mood, which I can't blame her for. She had a very different morning from her usual ones; she had a group of children around, she had new toys and games to discover, she had teachers to meet and a garden to play in, with sand and slides and swings. An absolute overload of information and stimulation for her brain to make sense of. But she did so well and so did I.

On the drive home she fell asleep, but woke up the second we got home, which gave Pixel the opportunity to show her how happy he was to have her back again. By then, Pixel and Molly were friends. I had no doubt about it. She was happy for him to sniff her toys; in fact, I saw her several times pick a toy up and pass it to him. He would sniff it and, if it was a particularly good smelling toy, he would give it a lick or pick it up. As far as I can remember, he never destroyed any of her toys. However, if Pixel had been that kind of dog that loves to kill all stuffed animals, I would have been there to swap one of Molly's toys for one of his instead and made sure to amuse him by playing with that toy, discarding Molly's one. I would have explained, time and time again, to Molly why we had to do that.

Pixel and Molly's friendship was based on mutual stroking: Molly liked to feel Pixel's fur under her hand and feet and Pixel liked sniffing her belly and licking her toes. This was absolutely gorgeous to see but was always done under active supervision. This is probably why I barely have any pictures of them together at that age- I was too busy just watching them all the time.

Their relationship was also based on food: Molly was a bit of a messy eater and would always drop food on the floor, Pixel loved sitting under her highchair and loved to just wait for the food to fall from the sky. In this case, I had to make sure she wasn't eating anything that could be harmful to Pixel, such as grapes, raisins, sweets, or any food with onions or leeks in them.

If she did have food with dangerous ingredients for Pixel, he would then be either on me while she ate, in the playpen, or in Gary's office. Another option was that I could have also kept him on the lead in the house, away from the area where Molly might have dropped food. Just like her toys, time and time again, I would tell Molly about food that Pixel could and couldn't eat.

I knew she was listening, because one day, I bought some raisins in little boxes, which she loved to eat while in her pushchair on longer walks. I was preparing her lunch box for preschool, and she told me to put the raisins in the lunch box, because Pixel wasn't at nursery with her, so she could eat them there. That was one of those moments of pure reward! Not only because Molly had learned to keep her furry brother safe, but other dogs too! The cherry on top of the cake was that Molly was the kind of kid to tell stuff like that to her little friends at preschool. She was mostly doing it to show off, I'm sure, but they would still hear it, and hopefully learn from it.

Not long after Molly had started nursery, we found the perfect home at the perfect price and our offer was accepted! So, on Valentine's Day 2014 we moved into our first home and gave Pixel the garden he had long deserved.

When purchasing a house in the UK, you enter a chain. You normally have to wait for the people you are buying a house from to find their next house, they will then wait for the current owners of that house to find their next living accommodation, and so on. However, we were lucky, because we were first-time buyers, we didn't have a to find someone to sell our property to and the people selling the house we wanted to buy had moved to France, so we didn't have to wait for anyone. However, the home-buying process is so long and stressful, it still took us about 2 months to get the key for our house!

Those 2 months were spent packing and going on Pinterest a lot! Molly was still little, but I would let her look at photos of other kids' bedrooms, so she could choose what colour her room would be. Eventually she decided on light purple!

I knew the move would be busy and difficult for Pixel to understand, moreover, both Gary and I would be very busy getting everything organised. So, I booked Molly in for an extra day at nursery and was glad to hear my parents-in-law were going to be around from London to help out. My father-in-law, John, was a plumber, but is now retired. He knew about properties, and I think he secretly-not-so-secretly loved a project. And our new house was definitely a project!

So, in the weeks leading up to the move, and right after we got the keys of the house, John and two of his workers came down to Dorset and started working on the house. We would go see them sometimes, have a look at how the changes were coming along and get Molly and Pixel used to the new place.

Pixel loved the garden! He would stay under the pergola if it was raining, or simply enjoy the freedom of coming in and out through the patio door, which was left open a lot. He'd figured out pretty fast where things were and loved having his own patch of grass to sniff and do whatever he wanted. Molly loved it too. We talked about what we would be planting or what toys she could have there, and she would suggest having picnics on the grass with Max! It was a very special moment in our life, even if it was very stressful and worrying, it was also something I knew that we would never experience again.

Our moving day came and went. Gary had hired a great moving company, and they were absolutely amazing. Somehow, they had all our life packed up in their lorry and unpacked again in our new place in no time. I can't even imagine how we would have done it without professionals like them sorting it all out for us and moving the heavy things, like the sofa, wardrobes, and desks.

Pixel was with us that day. At the flat, we got him in our car and went to the house, then we used the garden and the living room to keep him out of the way when the movers were bringing our belongings in. Looking back now, I can see how it would have been better for him to be somewhere else, as the whole thing must have been extremely confusing and distressing for our furry boy. But we were so excited to start this new chapter as a family and I really wanted to share that with him.

It was funny how in some ways, I felt like we owed him to live that moment with us. We had talked for so long about buying a place of our own, to give Pixel more space and a garden. I really feel like that milestone was like a moment in life dedicated to Pixel and what having him in our life meant.

Before you go thinking that our garden is the size of a football stadium, let me tell you that it really isn't. It's big enough to have a lovely summer house and do lots of outdoors activities, but it isn't massive by any means. But that was beside the point and Pixel always seemed to find something to sniff, or a good, yet rare, spot in the sun to sunbathe.

Decorating a house can be so much fun! It would be even more fun if you had an endless amount of money, which we didn't have, so we had a few visits at IKEA, kept some of the old furniture and got creative. We also got patient and held off on some things, while slowly bringing more money in. But, most importantly, we learned that when things go wrong at your own property, it sucks because you can't just call the landlord to sort it out. You are the landlord, you have to sort it out, you have to pay for everything that goes wrong with it. So, when the cooker died, we had to buy another right way. When the boiler needed changing, we had to get that sorted as quickly as possible. When we had very bad weather and the pagoda roof and the fences blew over and some pieces were broken, we had to get that fixed immediately ourselves.

In some ways, even after adopting a dog and having a child, it was owning a house that made both Gary and I realise we were grown-ups. We had all the responsibilities and worries of adulthood. And to be honest, I don't think either of us were ever expecting that, nor were we quite ready for it.

Who am I kidding? We are still not ready for it now!

Time passes, as it always does, and we had the magical event of celebrating Molly's 3rd birthday at the new house. We had family and friends over, which was somewhat of a novelty for us and Pixel. We are not reclusive, but we are also not the kind of people that love to socialise and have lots of people over all the time. In fact, we rarely had people over when I think about it. It wasn't us then, and it isn't us now.

But, for Molly's birthday, we had Gary's family and Grainne, Max, Maya and Eva, and some little friends Molly made at pre-school over with their mums. There were well over 15 people around, which was unheard of.

Pixel didn't know what to do with himself. He wanted to follow the kids, stay around the food, get cuddles from whoever was willing to pet him, and wanted a nap. It was all a bit much for him, not to mention that both Gary and I were busy entertaining, so we couldn't give him too much attention.

When it was time for the cake, which was followed by a fun pinata, we brought Pixel into the living room. He had his bed, water bowl, and scattered treats to find. Sniffing out those bits of food helped him to wind down a bit, as the party overstimulated his brain, and he needed help to relax.

Funny thing is... I felt guilty leaving him in there. I selfishly wanted him to be part of his sister's birthday, like the others. I wanted him to be in all the photos and videos, knowing he celebrated with us. But that was the mum in me and a way-too-human-way of thinking. He was safe in the living room; he had all he needed and what he needed the most was that time away from the people in a room that had peace and quiet.

The party carried on brilliantly and all the kids and adults had a good time chatting, laughing, and enjoying the gentle May sun. Pixel slept through the singing, cake eating, pinata hitting and more. If you had walked into the hallway, you would have heard him snoring away.

After our guests left, Molly was sad to see them go, but very happy with the day she had, while Pixel was well-rested, happy and ready for his dinner! As parents, we felt a sense of accomplishment for being able to give both of our kids (human and dog) the day they wanted and needed.

Key Points

Children, even when little, understand much more than we give them credit for. We just need to be persistent and consistent. Little kids tend to forget things that you've said, so we need to repeat the same things over and over. They are not being lazy, stubborn, or naughty. Nothing like that, their brain and body are simply developing and there is so much information to take in. As they are retaining new input, it requires prioritizing, or selecting what needs to be kept and what can be remembered later, as such.

So, as children physically grow, they have to understand how to move their body properly and safely, to come up with words, sentences and thoughts and ideas. So, remembering not to give all their toys to the dog is not exactly a priority to the child's brain. This, of course, is also up to the individual child. Maybe, if Molly had cared more for her toys, or if Pixel had destroyed her toys in the past, she would have likely remembered to keep the toys away from him. As I mentioned, this was not our situation, so Molly didn't have that worry to live with.

Sometimes, when the love for your dog is so incredibly overwhelming, you can't help thinking of your furry companion as your child too, it is difficult to remember that your dog-child has different needs from your human one. Human ones are so much easier to understand, because we can relate to them- most of the time anyway. The dog ones might be more challenging to understand as they're a different species, but when you put yourself in your dog's paws and analyze the situation from his point of view, it is rather easy to sympathize with him and do what is right by the dog.

Chapter 11:

Nothing Prepares You For This

Our home improvement had come to a bit of a halt as we approached the beginning of the summer. We had spent a lot of time and money on improving the house and we had to take a break to have more money in the bank and more time on our hands.

In the meantime, I turned 34 and the British summer seemed to have started; the sun was out more often than not, Grainne and I would take the kids to the beach some days and have ice cream at the park after pre-school some others.

Molly had also miraculously been accepted at the same nursery Max was attending in Compton Acres, so they both were having wonderful days at that idyllic place. During that time, I decided it was time to find a job. Translating bits and bobs wasn't paying much at all and I also wasn't feeling fulfilled or happy about doing that. I didn't know what I wanted to do, but it needed to be something flexible, as I needed to be able to be around for Molly.

Being a mum was still going to be my priority.

Teaching in schools was out of the question because it would have been too many hours, and it would have been impossible to be around for Molly. Also, I hadn't worked in schools in 4 years by then, the appeal of going back into a classroom had gone. So, I put my thinking-cap on while the summer was in full-swing and Gary's sister, Charlotte, came over to visit us from London. Charlotte was and still is the fun-aunt! She's younger, she is into games, she's fun and pretty and always smells and dresses nicely. Molly absolutely adores her! Charlotte (nicknamed Char) was also very loving to Pixel, who couldn't get enough of her!

When Char was staying with us, at the end of July, the weather was warm and lovely. We were often out as she visited and Pixel and Gary were often left alone while Gary worked and Pixel... well, was power napping, mostly.

This might sound a little gross, but Pixel had been throughout his life, an occasional 'farter'. Because of their flat-faces, Pugs tend to swallow more air when eating or drinking compared to dogs who have longer noses, so farting isn't unusual in brachycephalic breeds. Moreover, and I didn't know this back then, but the food he was on (a well-known brand of dry biscuits) was full of rubbish and he wasn't eating anything fresh or healthy enough.

When Char came to stay, it seemed like Pixel was farting even more than usual. Because it wasn't anything new, we would laugh about it and comment on how gross it all was. However, on July 29th the joke stopped being funny.

On that day, we all went shopping and left Pixel's home for a little while in the afternoon. When we came back, he was happy to see us and Gary let him out and gave him his dinner, but he refused it. We added some cheese to it, to entice him, but that also didn't work, which was unusual. He then started to walk 'funny', like his legs couldn't quite hold his weight. Gary took him to the garden, thinking he might need the toilet. He then called me, as I was upstairs getting Molly ready for her bath. When I came down, I was a little stressed by what was happening with Pixel, having to put the shopping away and sorting Molly out- I didn't know what to think.

Honestly, I thought maybe Gary was exaggerating the situation and Pixel was fine. Pixel was always fine. Pixel was my rock. He had to be fine. Only… he wasn't, and I could tell too. He couldn't walk unaided, his back paws had collapsed; he seemed unable to control his bladder, and he seemed to be looking at us asking for help. I honestly don't know if he was in any pain or not. He wasn't complaining as such, but he certainly looked confused.

I called the emergency vet, which luckily was only up the road from us, and they told us we had better bring him in. With everything that was happening, my mind was racing between giving Molly a bath and how to stay positive for Pixel. I felt so overwhelmed by it all. Even now, as I recall the events, they are flashing by so fast. I was never so grateful to have Charlotte around as I was that day because both Gary and I could go with Pixel, while Molly was safe with her aunt.

We told Molly that Pixel wasn't well and needed to see the vet. I knew then and I know now that Molly needed more information and more time to process it all, but Pixel didn't have the luxury of that time, and neither did we. I do believe that Charlotte answered some of Molly's questions, although there wasn't much to answer, as we didn't know what was wrong with Pixel yet.

By the time we left the house, however, Pixel couldn't walk at all, and we had to carry him to the car. He had also lost control of his bowels and bladder, so we had a towel around him, just in case. The vet took him in right away and told us they needed to run some tests. They were going to keep him in, and we were told to go home. They said that they would call us in due course that night, so we had to make sure to have our phone with us.

'Prepare yourself' the vet said as we were leaving.

It took me a minute to realise what she meant. But my brain refused to hear it, because, to this day, nobody can still answer a simple question for me 'How do we prepare ourselves to lose forever someone you love?' I don't remember what I told Pixel as we left. I am sure I gave him a little stroke, but I don't remember how his fur felt to the touch. I don't remember if he wagged his tail, like he had always done every time I gave him a cuddle.

The call came around 11pm, when a vet nurse told us we ought to go in to say goodbye. My hands were shaking, my brain couldn't connect with what was happening. Once again, I was grateful to have Charlotte there to look after Molly, as she slept upstairs.

When we got to the vet, they let us in a room and Pixel was laying on the floor on a mat. I lay right next to him, tears flooding down my eyes, so much so I couldn't see him clearly. I kept telling him I loved him and stroking him. Gary was also crying and looking at Pixel with the most intense sadness I have ever seen. A mixture of loss, pure love and, somewhat, gratitude for the friend Pixel had been to him. Even the vet standing there was in tears.

It really was hard to say goodbye.

'He's so cold', I said to the vet 'Why is he so cold?' I asked Gary, who, not knowing what to say, looked at the vet. Both of us were waiting to hear what she would say, if perhaps we could put a blanket on him. She looked so puzzled, then almost scared and her gaze kept moving from me to Gary, until she said, 'Weren't you told?'… 'Told what?'… 'He is…' she couldn't finish the sentence. She didn't have to. There wouldn't have been, and never shall be, any words that could tell us we had lost our boy forever.

And we never even got to say goodbye.

We were not there for his final moments. This is what hurts me the most.

Pixel was there for holidays, parties, birthdays, tears, new jobs, new homes, births, and sicknesses. He was there, always. And we weren't there when he needed us the most. It is still too hard to accept, even now, years after he died, I still can't think about it without feeling like my heart is breaking all over again.

How do you go back to life when life has changed so very completely? How do you tell your heart that it has to mend and your brain that it has to keep functioning and your child that she will never see her furry brother again?

If I had been more prepared, I probably would have handled it better, but I wasn't. Gary and I didn't expect Pixel to leave our family when he wasn't even 8 years old and hadn't shown signs of being ill. We didn't know what he died of, but the vet suspected it was due to undiagnosed cancer. We could have paid to have an autopsy but, really, what was the point? It was too late.

So, to this day, we don't know what really took our boy away from us and I don't regret not finding out, because I know nothing would have brought him back.

When Molly woke up the next morning it was early. I hadn't slept much at all, as I cried most of the night, my eyes were puffy, and I could barely look at Molly before I started crying again.

'Why are you crying, mummy?' she asked, ever so innocently, ever so blissfully unaware. I was envious of that precious time she still had, when she didn't know Pixel was no longer with us.

I couldn't speak. I couldn't tell her.

Gary was also in pieces, and he also had barely slept, and neither of us was ready for that moment. The thing I knew, or I felt I knew, was that understanding death is hard, almost impossible and that, for Molly, it was her first time experiencing it. I wanted her to understand that it was final and a sad thing to happen, but I didn't want her to be traumatized by it.

I can't remember the exact words I said to her, but as I sat on my bed and she was next to me, I reminded her that the night before we took Pixel to the vet. I told her that Pixel was sick and that we didn't know he was sick, nor did we know why. 'Sometimes doggies get sick, but they can't tell you they are not well. Pixel couldn't tell us, so we didn't know.' I really believe she understood that. With an adult, I wouldn't have had to say anything else. They would have understood or worked it out, but with a child you have to explain everything and expect more questions too.

Thing is, I couldn't bring myself to say anymore. I was crying too hard to be able to finish telling her what happened. Gary did.

My husband, who was also broken inside, who had also lost our beloved companion, was probably less emotional than me or, simply, he had to be strong because I wasn't, and he knew I needed him to be. He told her that Pixel was too sick, even the vet could not make him better. He told her that Pixel had passed away and that he was not coming back home anymore.

That, I am sure, she did not understand.

'Where is he?' she asked.

'He is at the vet surgery.' Gary replied.

'Why can't he come home?' she asked, not understanding the situation.

'Because he died' he replied, 'Pixel died.' He said it again, almost admitting it to himself. His voice was low, as if coming from a place his body didn't want to go to.

Molly, little as she was, could see our sadness, but couldn't feel it herself. Gary tried to explain a bit more, by telling her that when someone dies, they can't be with us anymore, so Pixel couldn't come and be with us like before.

'Where does Pixel go now?' she asked and, boy, that was an even more difficult question, for the answer is unknown to us all, isn't it? I'm not a very religious person, and neither is Gary, but we do like to think that there is something after death. Maybe not so much as Heaven and Hell, but that, perhaps we don't 'just' get this one life. So, I told her that Pixel had become a star in the sky and that we can get to talk to him every night if we want to. 'He will be in our heart and in our memory forever. We will never forget about him, but now he can only watch over us as a star.'

In the days that followed, Molly had become a sort of nurse for me. I couldn't stop crying and I missed Pixel terribly. I remember how one day we were going to meet up with Grainne and Max to take the kids to a play-cafe. That would have been the first proper outing since Pixel had passed away and my eyes were incredibly puffy, so I told Molly we were going to cut a cucumber and I would put some slices on my eyes, as apparently that helps to reduce the puffiness.

'Can you cut me some too, mummy?' she asked.

'Sure, but you don't have puffy eyes.' I pointed out, cutting a couple of extra slices.

'No, I want to eat them!' she said, almost stating the obvious and, so, I cut quite a few more. We went on the bed. I put my slices of cucumber on my eyes while she chatted away next to me, eating her cucumbers. It was such a sweet moment that made me appreciate just how wonderful she was and how beautifully oblivious she was of the deep impact death can have on someone.

The strange thing about growing children is that they have a funny way of remembering, or rather forgetting things. In fact, she would come back to me later in the day, or the next morning asking where Pixel was. She didn't do it many times at all, but she asked as if she had forgotten what had happened; or as if she wanted to make sure it did happen and that I would answer the same thing, which, of course, I did.

She would even check with Gary that what I had said was true, like going to him and saying, 'Mummy said Pixel isn't coming back home anymore.' Or 'Mummy said Pixel is a star now.' And then she would wait for Gary's reaction. I can still remember a late evening, at bedtime, I found her looking out her window, and I asked her, 'Molly, you are supposed to be in bed, what are you doing?' And, with all the innocence in the world, she replied, 'I'm saying goodnight to Pixel.'

While that could have easily been another excuse not to go to bed, I hugged her, and we both said goodnight to our lovely boy and told him how much we missed him. I hope Molly learned that we loved Pixel deeply. He was a dog, who to us was family, our first child. I can only hope that Molly will continue to feel so strongly about animals throughout her life and will always love and care for them, even more so when they live with her.

We talk about Pixel even now, that many years have passed. We remember his birthday and the anniversary of his death. His photos and portraits are still around the house and some of his ashes are beautifully kept in some pendants Grainne made for me.

Now, Molly doesn't really remember Pixel, but she still knows how much he was loved, and she fully understands how much he is still missed.

Key Points

When children ask about the dog, even if you had already told them many times that he is no longer coming back, and you have explained multiple times what happened, is part of the process a developing brain has to go through to absorb and learn something new. And the more difficult this new thing is, the more the brain has to work to accept it and make sense of it all.

Death is definitely a challenging notion for our brain to come to terms with and to understand, so expect it to take a while and for your child to ask confirmation of what happened, many times.

Grief hits people very differently. Some people cry more than others; some people show more anger than sadness; some feel a deeper attachment to a higher power, which helps them ease the pain. We are all different and this, I think, makes it harder to reach out to everyone and have rules to follow that will fit us all.

In all honesty, I feel that Gary and I handled it the best we could, and I don't regret anything.

My mother believed that I shouldn't have cried in front of my child. But I feel her perspective was because of the era and way she was raised. Back then, and still perhaps in some cultures, children are often kept ignorant on certain parts of life and parents are supposed to not show emotions, which I can understand. Us parents are meant to be our children's rock; we are meant to be strong enough to endure their pain and ours. However, Gary and I strongly believe that it is ok for Molly to know that we are always here for her, that we can be strong for her, and we will support her, always. But it is also good for her to know that it is ok to cry, it is ok to feel pain and sorrow.

All those feelings, all those tears do not make you a weaker person, nor do they make you less of a parent. I want her to grow up to know that having feelings, being sad, crying, grieving, all those things are part of life. They are all part of what makes us human.

Perhaps, and this is just my opinion, if our parents' generation were taught that it was perfectly acceptable to show our emotions, we wouldn't have as many mental health issues as we have now. Maybe, I wouldn't have suffered deep depression years before, nor would I still be suffering from anxiety to this day. It is taking me a long time to learn how it is ok to accept and feel my feelings such as that I get sad, that I can cry when something bad happens, that I can grieve the death of someone, especially my boy Pixel. But I do feel that listening to and feeling my feelings is helping me to understand my emotions better and to accept them.

I feel it was good for Molly to see us crying,

because it was a sad thing to happen and because we loved Pixel so dearly, that crying is a normal, even healthy, reaction to such a challenging situation. I also feel it was good for Molly to see her dad cry. Often, we are told that boys or men should not show such strong emotions and should not cry, which I find unnatural and unfair.

I believe it was educative for Molly to learn that death is part of life, even if it hurts and even when it feels like you have been robbed of someone incredibly precious to you.

I think it was part of Molly's learning to ask questions when they popped into her head and to, sometimes, not have an answer to those questions, simply because we don't really know what happens after we die.

Telling her that Pixel had become a star made us all feel better, it gave us hope and comfort. Is it the truth? I don't know! What happens to our souls after we die? I might have my belief and I'm sure you have yours, but what really happens we simply do not know - and I hope to keep it that way for a very, very long time.

Chapter 12:

Wilco

Is a house without a dog a home? I really don't think so.

Our house felt immensely empty without Pixel. He really left a void in our heart and life. I wasn't really thinking of adopting another dog. I wanted Pixel back. I wasn't ready to bring another dog into my life. As the thought of adopting another dog made me feel like I was simply replacing Pixel. What if Molly thought Pixel was dispensable? That you can just get another dog, and everything is fine?

Yet, two weeks after Pixel passed away, his breeder, Mrs Perret, with whom I shared the sad news as soon as it happened, got in touch to tell us that a young pug called Robert needed to be rehomed. His breeder was a show breeder in France, but deemed him not suitable for showing, and sold him to a woman in the South of England, about an hour away from where we live. Mrs Perret asked if we knew anyone who might want to adopt this little puppy or if, perhaps, we wanted to have him ourselves.

Obviously, I shared the email with Gary as soon as I read it. I can tell you that the moment I saw it, I wanted to rescue that dog. Gary, however, wasn't as convinced right away. His question, 'Isn't it too soon?' was legitimate and fair. Yet, I couldn't stop thinking about the little pug. So, I asked Gary if I could at least find out what the situation was before we fully decided against it, which he agreed to.

After many emails with the breeder, a few calls with the woman who had adopted Robert, and some detective work, we found out that the breeder was reputable and known in France for showing beautiful and healthy pugs (as healthy as pugs can be, anyway). We also found out that the woman who bought Robert already had a pug and wanted a sibling for him. However, she 'didn't expect the puppy to pee everywhere and to keep annoying the other dog'. Clearly, the woman didn't know about puppies! To 'solve the problem', she was keeping Robert isolated in a room while he was waiting to go to his new home.

I kept relaying all my findings about Robert to Gary and Molly, who was probably too little to understand, but whom I felt needed to know that, if we were to adopt this puppy, the decision had not to be taken lightly. Even though she was just a toddler, I wanted her to know that adopting a dog requires immense research, asking questions, speaking to a lot of people, and finding out as much as possible about the dog.

Even if a little of that process sank into Molly's developing brain, I am satisfied.

After two weeks of daily emails, calls and messages, we were ready to take Robert away from that woman (who should not have been allowed to have him in the first place) and to welcome this young puppy into our home.

Robert needed a fresh start. He was to become Wilco and to have a family who really loved him and who would dedicate time to teaching him where was the appropriate place to go to the toilet, to walk nicely with us and how to walk off lead but come back when called. He needed to know he was safe, that he would be regularly fed and have access to fresh water whenever he wanted.

He deserved a comfy bed for him to sleep in and toys to play with, along with humans that would be there for him. All things that he wasn't getting where he was at.

Not only did we want Wilco to have a great life because he deserved it, but also because children learn from us all the time. We wanted our daughter to learn to respect animals and understand how to give dogs a good life.

The only consolation I have ever had about Pixel's death was that his life had been amazing! He was loved, he had the best care we could offer, he had many (many) beds to sleep in, including ours; he had attention, care, playful times... he had everything a doggy (and human) could wish for. And we still had so, so much love to give, so why not offer it to Wilco? This unfortunate, skinny, little boy, who hadn't had much affection in his life so far, was to be treated so very differently in his new home. He was to become part of the family and loved just as much as the other members.

I seriously never understood why the breeder thought he wasn't handsome enough for showing, because Wilco was a gorgeous puppy pug.

As I explained at the start of this book, pugs can have many health problems, especially due to their flat-faces. Luckily Wilco's nose wasn't too flat, which meant it was easier for him to breathe. However, Wilco, like many pugs, had a double-curvy tail, which might cause problems to his spine, particularly in old age. Also, his right back paw was a 'bit funny' as he would appear to kick it more to the side when he walked.

As soon as we collected him from that woman, who never even bothered asking about him after we left, we took him to the vet to be checked. The vet declared him a healthy boy, but too skinny (an indication that the woman was underfeeding him). He didn't seem concerned about his back paw, so it might just have been the way he walked.

During the time of my dealings with Wilco's breeder and the woman who were looking to rehome him, my brother and his now-ex-wife were on holiday in England and were staying at our house. While their time with us might not have been the greatest, as I was still grieving, it was certainly handy, as we were able to go pick up Wilco, leaving Molly with them. I also hope their stay with us ended on a brighter note, as they got to meet Wilco too.

We prepared Molly for the arrival of our new puppy with excitement, but we really wanted to make sure she knew Wilco was not a substitute for Pixel. This is something both Gary and I felt very strongly about. We didn't want her to think that Pixel, or any other animal, could be dispensable or easily replaceable, because it was not the case.

'Pixel will always be special.' We told her many times, 'Wilco needs a family, because the person he is with now is not nice to him, but we will be nice, won't we?' It was important to us she knew the value of caring for a dog, and that she understood that Wilco needed us and needed our attention and love.

I remember Molly found it tricky to understand why this woman was not kind to Wilco, which was so difficult to explain, so I told her the truth 'I don't know why, Molly, but some people are not very nice, unfortunately. I don't like it when people aren't nice, that is why I like to be kind and I try not to be horrible to anyone, even when they make me angry. And that is why we also always tell you to be kind.' I could see her mind thinking and taking it all in, as her bright blue eyes would look at me and she would touch my hands.

When I think back about those conversations, because we did have many of that kind, I remember how I would feel the loss of Pixel particularly strongly. He would have been with us during those times. He would have been keeping us company, snoring away, or wanting a cuddle, so while my daughter was, and forever will be, my sweet little girl, I was struggling to enjoy life. I knew Pixel wasn't coming back and I couldn't do anything about it, but I had so much love to give to a dog.

My life was not complete without a dog in it, and that was absolutely clear to me. So, while I knew it might have been a little soon after Pixel left us, I also knew there was almost no other way to go about life without the companionship of a dog, at least not for me.

I needed Wilco and, it was very clear then, he needed us too.

Wilco came to us with a collar, a lead, all legitimate paperwork, his passport, and a few undisclosed behaviour issues, which I know now were caused by the way he was treated while with the woman who adopted him, but also by the way his life started with the breeder.

I wasn't a behaviourist or a trainer back then, so I didn't expect him to have as many behavioural issues as he did; I didn't know why he had them or how to help him. However, one thing was certain, Gary, Molly and I were going to give him the best life we could.

Wilco was cute, oh my gosh, he was adorable! He was just over 5 months old, so he wasn't super young, but still very much a puppy. He was curious, but also a little wary of things. However, one thing was obvious from the start, he loved people! He was very friendly with humans and would happily engage in long cuddle-sessions! Dogs also didn't seem to be a problem for him, in fact, he craved to play with other dogs, with a particular fondness for pugs.

When we got home, Molly was very excited, but we had prepared her beforehand, asking her to be as calm as she could muster, and to wait for the puppy to come to her, which he did in a matter of seconds! Not only his tail was wagging, but his whole body was too!

Sometime after this special moment, when I learned about dogs, I discovered that a waggy tail isn't always a happy tail, however, when a dog's tail wags along with his bottom and, in some breeds, big part of the lower part of the body, then that's one happy and excited dog.

The memories of that very first connection between Molly and Wilco are a bit of a blur, I know I had tears in my eyes, and I couldn't help but feel happy and sad at the same time. Happy because Wilco was now part of the family and seeing Molly with him was such a beautiful thing; sad because Pixel wasn't there to be part of it all.

We let Molly help as much as she could and wanted when introducing Wilco into our life. She had chosen his bed and the bowls he would drink and eat from. I needed everything to be different from what we were using for Pixel, some we bought new items.

She chose a couple of toys for him too, but the real fun was then going to our local pet shop with Wilco and seeing Molly picking some toys and asking him which one he liked best. It was so ridiculously cute, but also so important. Even little things like that meant that Molly was actively participating in Wilco's life and those interactions were bonding them in a safe and positive way.

On top of that, having our very excited daughter picking stuff for our new puppy helped to make it all a little less of a novelty. She had chosen everything and had seen where they should be placed in the house. While at first this was very exciting for her, the novelty of that new bed or new bowl quickly wore off- as happens with young children.

However, meeting Wilco for the first time at the house was an extremely exciting moment for Molly. I could see how she was struggling to keep it together and I am sure she wanted nothing more than to run up to Wilco and hug him and cover him in kisses, but she let him go up to her and, for that, I am grateful to our little girl. Promptly, we praised her for listening to us and for doing well by Wilco. This was something we always made sure we did. She deserved to know how amazingly well she was doing.

Wilco, however, was not prepared for a small human and all the amazing things that were about to happen to him, so he was excited and jumpy and didn't know how to contain himself. To be fair, we expected that. Not so much because we had a puppy before, but because if you have ever seen a puppy, you know they can be a little bonkers. However, we were going to address that and help Wilco to politely live in a world with humans, especially little ones.

My brother and his ex-partner left the day after Wilco came to live with us. While it was sad to see them go, it also gave us the opportunity to dedicate our time to our new puppy, which was extremely important.

Although Wilco had many comfy beds, initially he seemed to prefer sleeping with us. Molly had her room and was, by then, a good sleeper. We asked her to call us in the morning when she'd woken up, instead of just walking into our room. This was because we didn't know how Wilco would react to seeing her just walking in. Everything was new to him and while he really seemed to adore Molly, we didn't want to take our chances.

The first couple of mornings went beautifully and he was waking up to the sound of Molly's voice calling us, I would go get her and take her to see Wilco and sleepy Daddy on the big bed- everything was fun and cute. However, one morning, about four or five days after he arrived, the moment she walked into the room with me, Wilco got super excited as usual. As we were giggling seeing him so happy, he suddenly passed out! He fell to the side, laying there, not moving. I thought he was dead. Gary thought it too. We looked at each other in complete terror. And, for a second, nobody moved, nobody said anything. I honestly don't know what Molly thought, I don't think I had the time to formulate many theories myself before he got back up and appeared to be completely fine.

Immediately, I got on the phone with the vet, and we found out that Wilco had in fact fainted. He must have been so excited to see Molly, so happy to be there, that he simply fainted. This happened again a couple more times at the start of his life with us.

Wilco's behaviour was so different from Pixel's, which fascinated me. I thought all pugs would be the same and have the same kind of temperament and personality. All books we read on pugs lead us to believe that, anyway, but we were wrong, so, so very wrong. Wilco had his own likes and dislikes; he had his own personality and, no doubt due to his history, he had his issues.

Our main goal with Wilco was to make sure he was toilet trained, that he wouldn't chew Molly's stuff or Molly's body! And that he wouldn't jump up at her, or anyone else. We were very much focused on working on him, with the belief that dogs were the problem to solve when it came to having the perfect family dog. After all, that is kind of what we did with Pixel, so we expected to do the same with Wilco.

Oh boy, how wrong were we?

With Pixel we introduced a newborn baby to the house. A baby who couldn't walk up to the dog, who couldn't call the dog over, who couldn't touch toys, food, or anything else. A baby who wasn't even eating

149

food at first. So, clearly, every interaction would have been guided by us adults or by what the dog wanted.

This time around we were dealing with a whole new situation: Molly was over 3 years old, she could walk, run, skip, and jump, she was eating solid food and could even get some of it by herself (especially if left unattended). It seemed that Molly had more toys than Hamleys and loved leaving them everywhere. She was opinionated and wanted to be as independent as possible. She was a mini adult which was totally different from the little newborn baby we introduced Pixel to.

So, while we initially put all our efforts into Wilco's training, we came to realise that we were overlooking the other creature that needed training: our daughter! When we recognized that we had overlooked or taken for granted that Molly would know how to be around Wilco, just because we had Pixel before, we started to be more careful and more attentive towards her education about dogs. She was allowed to help us with his meals, she would fill the water bowl (making a right mess by the sink when she did), she got to choose the treats we were using to train him and helped celebrate him when he was learning to do his business outside.

Not knowing any better, we kept her from helping us with training him on behaviours we were learning at puppy class, and she never joined us during puppy school at the local dog training classes we were attending. Looking back, I wish she did join us. She was very little, but she could have already helped a lot! At puppy class, she would have seen how Wilco was interacting with other dogs and could have learned about how puppies played with each other, which is something she never experienced with Pixel.

The trainer we used was absolutely lovely and so very knowledgeable of dogs. She was a positive reinforcement trainer and never once made us or Wilco feel uncomfortable. We are very grateful for her teachings, I just wished there would have been more encouragement towards having children involved in the everyday training and life with dogs. At the time, I think it simply was not done; having kids in dog classes was not a normal event. In fact, it is still not explored enough, which I strongly believe it should be.

We don't give kids enough credit for what they can understand and do.

At the time, I didn't realise Molly could have helped us with training Wilco. Nor did I understand that it would have helped us parents, and it would have been beneficial for Wilco to know that Molly wasn't just a playmate, but she was someone to listen to, to respond to, to look up to. Moreover, it would have been really good for Molly, because she would have had that connection and interaction with Wilco, which she so very craved, but it would have been positive and educational way to build their relationship.

Key Points

If I could go back in time, I would start by training our daughter before adopting Wilco. I know we didn't have much time, but we could have taught her more about dogs and having a puppy, rather than expecting her to know stuff simply because she had Pixel in her life before.

Luckily, nothing went wrong between Molly and Wilco, but it could have, and it would have been far better and more useful to educate Molly about Wilco from the moment we had decided we were going to adopt him- before he even came into our home.

As mentioned above, I would also involve our daughter in more activities involving Wilco's training and general upbringing. For example, I would ask her what she wanted for Wilco to do with her or areas we could work on. Such as I would ask her to list the things he was doing that we didn't particularly like and work on helping him to do something else instead.

I would certainly help my daughter to learn about basic, but essential dog body language, so that we could understand our puppy more. If she and I knew dog body language, we could have understood what Wilco might not like or what might make him feel uncomfortable. Then we would have avoided doing those things- and done something else instead.

To be honest, going back, we should not have adopted Wilco as 'blindly' as we did with such a young child in the house. We didn't know what and who we were going to get and, despite all the issues that he came with, he loved Molly from the start. However, with a child around the house, he did endure more than he should have. Knowing what I know now, I thank our lucky stars that Wilco was so kind and gentle to her, even when we allowed more silliness around him than it was fair for him to live through.

In fact, when I talk to clients now or when I teach Kids Around Dogs® courses, I always point out to make sure families with children adopt a dog they had gotten to know before taking him or her into their home. I discourage families with children from adopting a dog blindly from abroad or other ways, like we did. Not everyone will be as lucky as we have been, and too often children and dogs are put into situations they cannot handle, or they don't like and don't know how to cope with.

Chapter 13:

Kids Around Puppies –
What We Trained Molly To Do

Whether or not kids and dogs share a home, we always need to remember that kids, especially when they're very little, learn what is right and wrong from us and our actions. All children look up to their parents, carers, or other adults that they like or love and mimic what they do. So, when we adopted Wilco, we wanted to make sure Molly knew where he came from, why we were going to adopt him, and that every dog deserves to be loved.

While it was very sad to know that little Wilco had gone through such difficult times before coming to us, every situation can be a lesson to teach our kids. We told Molly Wilco's story to help her feel empathy for her furry little new brother.

When she would ask questions like 'Why was that woman (previous owner) horrible to Wilco?', it was sometimes difficult to keep anger and hatred for that woman, and others like her, at bay. However, an appropriate and calming answer is a better way to deal with it. Also, an honest one.

I would often answer something along the line of 'Sadly, some people don't care for dogs the way they should. Some people don't feel enough love for them, so they don't think dogs deserve or need as much love and care as we will give him.' She was still very little, so she would often ask the same questions multiple times, as if to confirm what she had been told before, and for her developing brain to retain that information, eventually.

I believe it is beneficial when raising children, even at a very young age, to tell them as much as possible how we should respect and treat animals. This way, as they grow up, they have this knowledge ingrained in them- it simply becomes a part of who they are. One of the many positive things about adopting a dog is how you can teach your kids to always be patient and kind to dogs, because some problems can't be solved quickly.

As we were helping Wilco settle into his new life with us, Molly certainly noticed the importance of being kind and patient with him. We made sure Molly was as involved as possible and all her interactions and little tasks involving Wilco were age appropriate. Such as when it came to toilet training Wilco, Molly happily joined in while celebrating every wee and poo outdoors. When he had accidentally toileted indoors, we would just clean it up, and move on without telling him off or making it into a big deal. If he did toilet indoors, it was simply because we weren't organised enough and forgot to take him out when we needed to.

Sometimes we had to remind Molly not to worry if Wilco had a wee or a poo indoors, as she would get agitated when that happened, but at the same time she knew we would take care of it, so that helped her to feel reassured. Also, by helping us with rewarding Wilco for doing his business outside, she felt involved, which I strongly believe helped her to feel more in control of the new and somewhat out of the ordinary situation. When you think about it, we know that people don't just stand up and go toilet in the middle of the living room, right? We understand it is strange, and children get that too.

Even when children learn to go potty and you have portable potties in every room of the house, there is still a specific place where children learn to go- the toilet or portably potty. They don't just do their business on the rug, stairs, or random places on the floor. So, if the dog wees in the house, children know it's not right and, some children more than others, would feel strongly about it and will want to rectify that situation. One thing we did with Molly, and I recommend is to tell children to inform the parents or other grownups and by getting them to help us instead of scolding the dog. By doing this, we can give the child control over a situation they view as different and perhaps even unacceptable.

Jumping up for Wilco was great fun! By jumping up, especially at Molly or Max, who was still visiting us regularly, he would get them to scream, run and just activate the crazy-button all kids have. Wilco loved that! And, I think that to a certain extent, so did Molly, who would sometimes try to get Wilco to chase her. While it is general knowledge to tell the kids not to run or scream, it is actually the hardest part and so difficult for them to do, because it is a natural instinct and part of self-preservation. Moreover, often, children simply don't know what else to do. They can't run, scream, climb stuff or anything else that would attract attention to themselves, so what should they be doing instead?

They can do the 'Be a Statue' instead.

What to do: Teach your kids to stand still, cross their arms over their chest and lower their heads to either look at their crossed arms, or to close their eyes. This will tell the dogs that they are boring and nothing to be too interested in, prompting the dog to move away.

Why does this work?

By standing still the dog will not be tempted to run after the children or chase them.

By crossing their arms over their chest the kids will be less tempted to fidget and to move their fingers in a way that might be interesting to dogs

By looking down or closing their eyes, the kids will not be making eye contact with dogs.

Generally speaking, dogs don't like to make eye contact, as it can be seen as a confrontational situation to them. Even if a lot more dogs are adapting to our human ways of staring at each other, most dogs are still learning or evolving and might not like that.

When kids and dogs chase each other, as so often happens and as I mentioned before, it can sometimes just be a way for them to play. And while it looks like fun, it isn't always the best way for the two to interact and can be very dangerous. Young children are still a little wobbly on their feet and tend to fall a lot. If that happens while the dog chases them, they might feel the dog made it happen (so it's the dog's fault) or the dog might jump at or onto the child on the floor, which might even lead to over excitement from the dog, often displayed in the form of little nibbles to the skin and some scratching. Even if the dog does this in a friendly and playful manner, it can still hurt the child, making the dog appear 'bad', 'naughty' or, God forgive 'aggressive'.

Teaching the kids to play with the dog can be such a rewarding and fun experience! Moreover, it can avoid preventing misunderstanding situations like the one described above.

I highly recommend getting a long tug toy or a flirt pole, because those toys have a long lead attached to a fluffy plushy or a ball or something similar to attract the dog to play with. By using these toys, your hands, or the hands of your child, are holding the end of the lead or a rope, at a safe distance from the puppy teeth, which are way too busy chewing on that attached toy.

Why are these kind of tug toys fantastic for child-dog safe interactions?

- They are helpful for those times when your puppy wants to chew on everything in sight

- They are great to distract your dog from doing things you don't want him to

- They are a fun way for the dog and human to bond

- It helps the dog to have a more enriched life, by also stimulating the brain in a positive way

And the cherry on top of the cake? The kids love it too! They will know they can play with the dog in a safe way! If you have your child involved, they can get to choose the colours of the toy, how the toy attached to the long rope, or they can even make a tug toy themselves out of old clothes and/or recycling materials. Also, if the dog takes the children's toys, you and your kids can keep calm, because you know you can go get the dog's 'fun' toy and play with it and the dog will be far more interested in playing with his humans and his toy, rather than getting no attention and no reinforcement from stealing one of the children's toys.

It's an absolute win!

However, it is also important to remember that not having your children's toys everywhere at reach of the dog is a massive help to prevent the dog being tempted to grab what he shouldn't have.

Key Points

We need to remember that little kids copy what we do, but also enjoy what they are doing. If your children do something like chasing the dog who has stolen a toy, they might be a little annoyed by the toy being stolen, but they might also really like chasing the dog around. By letting it happen, or doing it ourselves, we effectively and constantly reinforce that behaviour, not only from the dog, but the child too.

I feel we take for granted how our kids should or should not treat dogs. There is always the idea that dogs need to learn to be around kids; that dogs are the dangerous ones. But what about teaching our children to respect dogs?

For example, you can teach children:

- Not to climb on dogs
- Not to disturb dogs while they are eating or sleeping
- Not to annoy dogs when they don't want to play
- Not to pet dogs when they don't want to be petted

All those situations can be upsetting for dogs, just as they would be upsetting for children. Respect and understanding should go both ways. But, when children are too young to fully comprehend these rules, it's our job as parents or carers, to make sure that we prevent certain behaviours, by managing situations and avoiding unsafe behaviours from occurring.

I said it before, but I will say it again, the best way to make sure everything goes smoothly between kids and dogs is by actively supervising and managing every situation, with stairgates, playpens, or the use of spare rooms. However, please, remember that those are spaces for the dog to go to while the kids run wild and you don't have the time to actively supervise, and should always be happy places, not places of punishment. The dogs should know that in these places, life is good, they might get a yummy bone in there, or some enriching toy (like West Paws, LickiMat, or Kong). The training for the 'dog nook' has to be done properly, and we'll see that later.

I also suggest giving your children, even the little ones, something to do instead of disturbing the dog. When they are babies and toddlers their abilities are limited, of course, but when they are more able to do stuff, get them involved! Get them to help you with training, even if it's just by throwing some treats on the floor for the dog to sniff out. By doing that, the dog can learn that, around your little child, food and all good things appear on the floor, so there is less chance of the dog feeling tempted to jump up.

When walking on the lead, you can use a Stormridge lead (an almost circular-like lead) that has a handle in the middle. So, you can hold the handle in the middle while your little one can safely hold the handle at the end of the lead, attached to the dog. If the dog were to pull, you will feel it, but your child will not. That means that the little human will be safe, but also feel involved in the activity with the dog, making walks less stressful too.

Children want to experience things. Stopping them from exploring everything and anything can be a real challenge and, sometimes, it's simply not helpful. Getting them involved, safely and always under supervision, can make your and their life so much easier and fun!

However, it is also important to remember that we don't want children to become scared of dogs because of the energetic behaviours puppies can have or in our attempts to stop the child from going crazy-bonkers around dogs.

In 2020, I developed a successful protocol to overcome the fear of dogs in kids and in 2023, I designed a protocol to help adults, too. You can read about it on the KAD website!

Over time, I learned what to say and what to avoid telling kids around dogs who are overexcited or agitated, like Wilco could get at times. And, while this book isn't about the phobia of dogs, I can tell you to never underestimate the child's fear. So, saying things like 'Don't be silly, it's just a little dog' is not helpful. What can go a long way is helping kids to understand dogs, their body language and how they feel.

Typically, children under the age of 4 find it difficult to understand feelings and understand that others have feelings that might be different from theirs is even harder. So, lower your expectations and know that your child isn't being difficult or insensitive, but she simply doesn't have yet the ability to comprehend emotions in the way we do.

Still, you can start planting the seeds of educating your children to know that dogs feel happy and sad too. Keep things simple and get ready to repeat yourself a lot; it's all part of the process and, you will see- it will be worth it!

Chapter 14:

Puppies Around Kids –

What We Trained Wilco To Do

When Wilco arrived, the biggest issue we had to overcome was the fact that he loved to jump up and grab stuff with his very sharp puppy teeth. It was like having a shark around the house! He had already lost some of his puppy teeth, but the teething phase was far from over. Some days, we could tell his teeth were driving him crazier than others. Not only were his gums darker than usual, but he was also on a desperate hunt for stuff to chew. Unfortunately, more often than not, our hands and feet were his preferred choice.

He also loved, and I mean, LOVED grabbing hold of Molly's dressing gown and pulling it around the house- while she was still wearing it! I will let you imagine the chaos that brought to our house in the morning! Like life wasn't already hectic enough!

The jumping up was also ridiculous! Those little legs were like springs and Wilco was not afraid of using them! He could jump surprisingly high, which might have been fun to watch, if you weren't the one that he was jumping at!

Wilco was also a bit of a puller on the lead, which didn't surprise us, as he had not been taken out for walks when he lived with his previous owner. So, the poor boy didn't really know what to do with a lead and a harness, and his brain was going a million miles per hour every time he was outside.

At that woman's home, he was locked in a room without enough food to eat for some time. When we picked him up and brought him home, we noticed how due to this he ate his food at the speed of light and with obvious worry that it would be taken away from him or that he wouldn't have more food later. For instance, he would take a bit of his food and then move it a little away, as if to hide the food from whoever was in the kitchen with him. Also, he ate his own poo, which he likely had done before to survive when food was scarce, and he was confined to that room.

Dogs, just like humans, have incredibly strong survival instincts.

Even though he had several behavioural issues, he had some great qualities too. He was, and still is, a cuddle bunny! He loves sitting on us, or on our feet and getting stroked! If you stop, he moves closer or scratches your arm or leg to ask for more. If he had the choice, he would have cuddles for hours! Incredibly, he was really good at being left alone, which was so important for me, as I had the pre-school run to do. Also, Molly had some activities, like swimming and dancing, so I had to be away a bit during the day. We never left him too long, especially at the beginning, when he was still only 5 months old, and everything was new to him. However, we quickly realised that being left alone for a bit was not a problem at all for him, and still isn't.

Because of his affectionate disposition, it was clear that he loved us- a lot! That love was reflected in him being brilliant at coming to us when called! Whether outside at the park, or around the house, whenever we called him, he'd come running, with his cute velvety ears flopping around by his face and his soft pink tongue dangling happily as he reached for whoever called him. Training him to recall was a breeze!

As I mentioned, food was life for Wilco, which helped massively when training him, as he would do just about anything for that bit of chicken or ham or whatever else we had to give him. To make sure we were doing everything right, we started puppy classes with a local positive dog trainer who came highly recommended, was really good, humane, and extremely knowledgeable of dogs- the amazing Denise Nuttall.

With Pixel in Switzerland, we learned our lesson from the bad training class that we attended and abandoned, and we were not going to fall for those methods again. We believed, and forever will do, that there are better ways to educate dogs. We didn't want to hurt our puppy, we didn't want to shout at him, we didn't want to use tools that would cause him harm or that would scare him into doing what we wanted. We wanted our dog to love us, not to fear us!

We were also raising Molly that way, why should it have been different for our dog?

Denise's puppy classes helped us to keep us on track during the lessons. It was a huge contrast to the training we had with Pixel. This time, going to class with a positive reinforcement trainer helped us remember most things and showed us that it was an experience we were missing in our life with Wilco. More importantly, it was an enriching experience for Wilco, who enjoyed learning, bonding and meeting other pups.

Toilet training was something we wanted to get started on right away, so we stocked up on yummy treats and were always ready to deliver one or two as soon as he finished doing his business outside. Because Wilco hadn't been fed properly with the previous owner, he had developed the unhealthy habit of eating his own poo. This is known as coprophagia, which is impossible to pronounce- but you are welcome to give it a try!

Coprophagia can be due to a few factors, including:
- A lack of proper nutrition
- Fear of being punished for pooing
- A lack of food
- When the dog doesn't see any other solution but eating what he creates to survive.
- It can also, eventually, become a habit, so the dog eats it just because he's always done it, he's used to it and he might like it, of course.

In Wilco's case I believe it was a few things: we knew that he wasn't fed properly, so his little body was likely lacking the required nutrients, which he tried to find in his own faeces. He was also underfed, which might have led him to eat his own faeces to survive. From our correspondence, I know the woman who originally adopted him didn't care for him much at all, so it could be possible that she had punished him for going to the toilet indoors, causing him to be stressed and fearful and eat the 'evidence', in order to prevent her from getting angry at him.

Despite our perceived grossness of coprophagia, it is just one of the behaviours that remind us of how resourceful and clever dogs are.

To help Wilco move away from this unhealthy behaviour, we had to be absolutely on the ball with his toilet training. We had to make sure to be there every time he pooed, so that we could reward him immediately, therefore distracting him from what he had just done, and pick up the poo right away, while he was busy eating something he was allowed to have. We always used training treats that tasted and smelled incredibly tempting to him, like small bits of cheese or chicken, which he absolutely adored. We had to keep at toilet training for a good length of time and even to this day, sometimes I feel he needs to be reminded that his poo isn't that interesting after all.

When it came to training Wilco to keep his paws on the floor and not jump up like a kangaroo, we first made sure Molly knew to keep calm. With Molly, we practiced the 'Be a Statue' pose, and showed her how to use long tug toys, so Wilco would stay on the ground while playing with her. However, there was more we could have done, and I will cover below.

A few training points that I missed were:

1. When the training children side of things was covered, we needed to concentrate on teaching our dog that good stuff will happen on the floor and only when all of their 4 paws are on the ground. This is key to educating dogs not to jump up at people in general, not just children. The main aim was to prevent the dogs from jumping up in the first place, because prevention is always better than cure!

2. Work on rewarding the dogs on the floor by always putting treats on the floor, rather than feeding the dogs on higher surfaces, unless they are eating their food from a bowl, which is better when a little raised.

3. Teach your dog to sit, lay down, or stand with all paws on the ground! This might sound obvious, but trust me, it isn't.

When we were training Wilco, a mistake we made was to ask him to sit, which he would do. But then we would reward him while his front paws were slightly lifting from the floor. We continued the mistake when he was standing- instead of rewarding him while all of his paws were on the ground, we would either reward him too soon or too late, and his front paws were already lifting a little or a lot. Getting the timing right was essential, but also tricky to do! Especially when children were around. Because Wilco would often get overexcited, we would panic and get worried that he might jump at the kids, and it would all go slightly wrong.

It is also worth considering training your dog to lay down rather than sit. This is to avoid bad timing, as you can easily see if the dog is no longer laying down, making it easier to get it right. Moreover, when a dog is laying down, he is at a lower height, which is better when living with small humans. Finally, dogs like to preserve energy, generally speaking, so if they are laying down, it would take them slightly more effort to stand up. They would think about it twice. If they really want to, they will stand up, but if they think it isn't really worth it, they will keep that position of laying down. You could place a few treats on the floor between their paws to make that 'down' position last longer.

What I wish I did right, or that I knew from the beginning, was to work with Wilco by myself first, in a relatively quiet place, like our kitchen or living room, while Molly was at nursery or asleep. I would then build up the difficulty of it all, by training outside in the garden, or with the tv on; and then out the front door, until we were ready to try more challenging locations, and with Molly present too, then eventually, we could add more distractions, like having other kids around. But building it all slowly and at the time Wilco needed, not the time I wanted him to learn.

I wish I had known about feeding him on the floor all the time, because I didn't back then. So, we were always feeding him hand to mouth, but if we had thrown or placed the treat on the floor, he wouldn't have had to jump or raise his paws at all, and the timing-issue wouldn't have been an issue at all! Not to mention that Molly could have then helped us sooner and, I think, he would have also learned much faster, with less frustration and less unsuccessful attempts.

Wilco, just like every puppy out there, went through phases of teething, which can be super challenging, because he would get hold of anything, whether they were his toys or Molly's. He also loved grabbing kitchen towels, shoes, and even socks with our feet still in them; our clothes, while we were still wearing them; our hands, hair, you name it, he would nip at. At first, we were slightly concerned: we knew puppies were bitey, as their puppy teeth were leaving to make space for adult-teeth. We also knew that dogs felt with their mouth, so it was somewhat natural for Wilco to pick stuff up with his mouth too.

But he seemed to be particularly relentless with Molly, who was having none of it. She would scream like a banshee to let the entire world know Wilco was pulling her clothes, or he was trying to get one of her toys, or whatever. She would also try to run away with the item Wilco was so desperate to have, all resorting in Wilco getting even more excited and interested in those items, with the added frustration and worry that stuff was getting taken away from him.

One day, after another silly chase to get one of Molly's toys back from Wilco, all the books I had been reading about dogs, and all the questions I had been asking in puppy class came to mind and I realised why Wilco was so keen on chasing Molly and having whatever item she had; and how to help him be relaxed around his toys… it wasn't the toy, and it wasn't Wilco fault, but it was the fact that whenever he would chew on our body parts, or he would take something that didn't belong to him, he would get a really strong reaction from us, like running away, screaming, even laughing, you name it!

It wasn't about him doing whatever he wanted, but it was about the fun he was having when those situations would come up. Molly running away while he chased her; or being chased when he had something in his mouth was so much fun and was making him feel good, reinforcing him to do it again and again.

I know I discussed the child-side of things in the previous chapter, so make sure to review that if needed, however we also need to help the dog to know how to behave. Chasing can be great fun for dogs, and they should have a bit of fun, right? So, they can chase things, just not the kids! Long tug toys can be used by adults too, so why not getting the dog to chase those instead? Perhaps use different tug toys than the one the kids are using, so the dog can differentiate the toys and will know that with the ones you are using, he can be a little more bonkers; while with the ones the kids are using, it is less insane.

Whatever you do, I recommend not to encourage the dog to chase a person, but just the toy! So, if you are holding a long tug toy, drag it to the floor and the dog starts chasing it, that's brilliant, let him do that and get hold of it sometimes. But do that while standing still, or sitting down, without walking or running anywhere. If you walk or run, while playing the game, the dog will associate your movement and the tug toy movement, with excitement and fun, but we want to discourage that, as it can teach the dog that it's ok to chase people too.

Should the dog chase you or the kids, while still working on this issue or because they have gone over their threshold of excitement, remember you too can stop and assume the 'Be a statue' pose.

We had discussed some things when we adopted Pixel, but we had simply forgotten. Probably because it didn't seem that important at the time, but when faced with a puppy and a 3-year-old running around while the kid screams like mad, well... suddenly you see that a situation like that isn't ideal, or acceptable or, quite possibly, even safe. So, we went back to work a lot on recall and kept Molly away from Wilco when he was in one of his excitable moods.

What we were doing, effectively, was managing the situation, which we did for a rather long time.

What I know now, and wish I knew then, I am sharing with you to hopefully help you on your parenting journey for children around dogs- is that puppies need to chew! Chewing is critical for a puppy's mental and physical development. When puppies mouth us, they often don't understand that they are hurting us at times, or they don't know that some chewing is more appropriate than others. This is why we need to teach them- train them, if you will.

Stock up on items that your puppy can chew, like bones, stuffed toys (WestPaws or Kong), puzzle toys, and long tug toys. You want to make sure to have stuff like that around the house in different rooms so they can be easily grabbed before your puppy decides it's time to chew on your stuff or your skin. Involve your kids in this too, because you want to make sure the puppy knows how to listen and respond to your children. Moreover, you will give the kids something positive and appropriate to do, rather than panic and freak out every time the puppy grabs hold of something that doesn't belong to him.

When you start to think your puppy might want to chew on something, ideally before they do it, get one of his toys and make the toy super interesting for the dog. For example, you decide to give your dog a buffalo horn. You could just chuck it on the floor and go 'Here you go'! Your dog will likely sniff at it for a bit, maybe chew it a little, but then follow you again. That is simply because the chew item, for as fun as it might be, isn't as interesting as you are when he chews you or your kids. So, instead of just giving your puppy the chew toy, play with it! Make it interesting, make it fun! And stay with your pup for a bit while he's discovering the new chew item or new to him, anyway. If your dog isn't keen to play with the toy, up your game and get something better, such as a pre-prepared Kong from the freezer or a bone.

Loose lead walking is also something that we had to work on with Wilco. By the time we adopted him, Molly no longer needed her pushchair, although we still had it for those 'lazy walks', but barely used it anymore. Molly was a rather independent child, but she also liked her comfort. That meant we had to be prepared for just about anything when leaving the house as anything could happen. Will she be walking by herself the whole time? In which case we needed her body harness only. Will she want to be pushed in the pushchair? In that case, we had to bring the pushchair too.

More often than not, she wanted to walk by herself, then would get bored or tired and wanted to be picked up. She would also refuse the pushchair and nothing else would please her but being carried by either me or Gary. As we were learning about her likes and dislikes, which she taught us quickly enough, we learned not to even bother with the pushchair anymore, so Wilco was never trained to walk by it. We also knew we didn't want any more children, so the pushchair ended up in the shed at the back of the garden for a while, until I gave it away.

When training Wilco to walk with us, the problem we were having was that he always wanted to walk between our legs or feet! When he did this, we would move away, but he would sneak back and walk between our legs again! We didn't know then that Wilco was doing this behaviour because of his anxious disposition and his actions were telling us that he felt safe. He mostly did it with me, but if I wasn't around, he would redirect his attention to Gary. Only rarely did he do this with Molly- luckily, as he could have tripped her over! It turns out, it isn't easy to walk with a dog between your legs.

As mentioned, at the time, we didn't know why Wilco would much rather walk between our legs than by our side. We assumed it was a lack of training or because he hadn't been taken out much or at all before reaching the UK, or that he simply didn't know how to walk nicely.

From the force-free classes we were taking with Denise, and the memories we had of training Pixel, we made sure to use a normal lead and not a retractable one. Wilco's lead was about a meter long, so it wasn't too short and or too long. Its length helped us to know what a good distance and space he should have during lead-walking.

We remembered to never keep walking when he was pulling and to reward him for walking with us. Wilco was a clever boy; loved to please us and lived for food, so it didn't take him long to figure out that walking with us would get him super yummy treats. Soon he would walk with us more and more. However, at any given opportunity, he would quickly sit or walk between my legs.

As time moved on, and I got more interested in learning about dog training and behaviour, I learned more about him, about his personality and about his preferences. I also came to understand more about his anxiety. Due to his traumatic early life experiences, Wilco was an anxious dog and he needed us to remind him that, now, he was safe, and his life was different from the one he had before. We were so desperate for him to learn that he was loved and forever will be. The thing is, when a dog, just like a human, has lived through difficult times, they can be left with lifelong trauma from it. At times, they might think that everything and everyone will make them feel like they did before. There might even be things or smells, sounds, or situations that remind them of the bad times they had and will trigger painful memories, making the traumatic experience resurface.

What exactly would trigger the anxiety when out walking, I couldn't tell you. Was it the big areas we were taking him to? Was it the wet grass he was walking on? But that couldn't have been, because he displayed his anxiety wherever we were- at the beach, side of the road, open grass. We couldn't work it out, but what we could do was help him feel secure with us. So, we kept training him to walk by our side when on the lead, adding another precious reinforcement to our training- sniffing the ground by our side. In fact, sniffing isn't just a way for dogs to find out about the world around them; but it is a wonderful way for dogs to use their brain in a positive way, helping them to relax and, ultimately, to reduce their anxiety.

We started by throwing some food on the floor or grass by our side for Wilco to sniff out and eat, instead of him trying to walk between our legs. However, if we were too late, he would sneak between our legs. Instead of leaving him alone, we simply stopped walking and encouraged him to smell some of the treats we had. So, he would follow the scent of the food in our hands, which would lure him to walk by our side instead of between our legs. Once he arrived next to our legs, we would put the treats on the floor for him to eat. He would be told what an awesome boy he was, in a calming voice, so as not to excite him. Then, we would give him time to sniff the food and find all the treats. Sometimes, we would add more treats, to give him extra time to almost 'reset' his brain from super anxious to calmer, as some days it would take him longer to decompress.

Key Points

While I am grateful you are reading this book and I hope you find it useful, nothing ever replaces working with a qualified, force-free professional. This trainer gets to meet you, your family, and your dog. They take the time to understand your lifestyle, your needs and your wants, will match them with your dog's needs and wants and then will plan accordingly.

When hiring a professional you want someone that is qualified to work with dogs, of course, but that also one who understands and wants to work with children, even the very little ones. This is one of the biggest reasons why I founded Kids Around Dogs®, because not all qualified dog professionals know how to work with kids and, still to this day, some simply don't want to work with kids.

I know we are all different and some people are simply not that inclined to work with little humans, however dogs share a world with children. So, I feel it is important to know how dogs and kids can live happily, safely and in harmony together, even if they don't share the same house.

When training your dog, please, remember to be patient and know that it might take longer than you think. Also, your dog might learn some cues super quickly and others a little slower. This doesn't mean that he can't do something or that he's been stubborn, lazy, or whatever. It might be that he finds one behaviour particularly rewarding, even if it is something that you don't like, so it is harder to stop doing it. Or it could be that he doesn't really understand what you are asking him to do instead. I recommend when this happens, that you and your dog pause and take a step back in your training. Make it simpler and slower for your dog and make sure you know what you are doing. This way, both you and your dog can work in synchrony to achieve your goal.

When training, it is also important that you learn basic dog body language, to help you understand what your dog enjoys and what he doesn't.

Check out some body language information at the end of this book!

Chapter 15:
Training Tips and Methods

As I've mentioned a few hundred times in the book, I am a firm believer in training without the use of punishment. None of my methods will hurt the dog physically or emotionally. I also don't use tools that could hurt dogs, nor do I shout at them.

Honestly, there is no need to be horrible to our beloved dogs.

Firstly, understand what your dog really loves! You can use food, if your dog loves food, as it is a faster way to reward your dog for doing well. But some dogs love a little play or toys more than food, while others love a bum-scratch more than anything.

What does your dog really, and I mean, really love?

I can tell you that Pixel loved cheese a lot (and I mean, a lot!), while Wilco would do just about anything for chicken! So, when training Wilco, I cut up some cooked chicken in tiny pieces, around pea-sizes and placed them in my training pouch, ready to get out at the right time. You don't want to be messing about with bags, tupperwares, pockets and all that. An easy training pouch strapped around your waist is the perfect solution.

You will also need to use something called a 'marker', which is either a clicker or a word that your dog will associate with doing the behaviour that you want him to do. When working with babies, toddlers, and dogs, the clicker is still a good idea, as it is simple and tangible. But, if you have a pre-schooler, it might be best to stick to a marker word. That is because the child will want to use the clicker and drive you insane if you don't let her. And, if the kid gets hold of the clicker, they will just be clicking all day, for just about anything, driving you insane and confusing the dog, ultimately defeating the purpose of training with a clicker all together.

Let's say you have chosen a word to be your marker. It should be something short, like 'Yes', or 'Good'. I heard someone saying 'Bravo!', which I still wonder if they continue to use because they wanted to show me they knew some Italian, or if it was their intention all along- still, that one works too.

Let's say your marker word is 'Good', as this is the most common one people use.

When you say your marker word, 'Good', it always needs to be immediately followed by a treat, so be mindful when to use that word. And remember, it is followed by a treat or whatever reinforces your dog, because you want the dog to know that he's done well, therefore he gets a reward.

Now that you have your pouch with some pea-sized chicken (reward) in it and have your marker word 'Good', you are ready to get started.

The 3D of training: Distractions, Distance, Duration.

Every trainer learns about the 3Ds, because they help us and the dog to learn gradually and with all the necessary steps and obstacles life puts in front of you and your dog all the time.

Distractions:

When first training something new, make sure you start somewhere super easy and neutral, like your kitchen or living room. It is just you and your dog, no TV, no radio, or other distractions. Turn your phone on silent!

Distance:

You will be starting near your dog, who might or might not be wearing a harness. He could sometimes have that on, and other times not, so that he gets used to both scenarios.

Duration:

There is no need to tease your dog and make him wait too long for his reward at first. In fact, the second that he does what you have asked him to do, you should say 'Good' and reward immediately after. Don't wait!

All the 3Ds will help you and your dog start at the easiest setting possible- so your dog can be confident in what they learn. Then, over time gradually increase the 3Ds to make things more challenging. But you can't move to a more difficult stage until your dog reliably responds at the easier stage first.

Basically, you can't run before you can walk. This is true for babies who start walking too, right?

Here is how to train the behaviours that I have mentioned throughout the book.

Sit or Down:

When it comes to big dogs, I prefer to teach 'Down' rather than 'Sit', as the dog might be so big as to reach the head of a child when sitting, but it is much less likely to happen when in a 'down' position.

This is also why I named this book 'It started with a Sit', because I see way too many caregivers repeatedly asking their dog to sit in extremely stressful situations or when forcing or asking their dog to sit in a potentially dangerous, stressful, or triggering situation for the dog. So, while I still teach the 'Sit' at times, I also want you to know that it should not be overused.

How to Train 'Sit'

1. Have some chicken in your hand and make a fist.

2. Get the dog to sniff the hand with the treat.

3. Keep your hand at the height of the dog, not higher, as we don't want the dog to jump.

4. After you are sure the dog's nose is interested in your hand, move your hand towards the back of the dog, in a slightly arched line from the nose towards the back or tail.

5. We want the dog to follow your hand, because if he does, his bottom will automatically hit the floor and the dog will be in a sitting position.

6. As soon as the dog's bottom is on the floor, use your cue word 'Sit'.

7. Mark the behaviour by saying 'Good'.

8. Reward the dog by letting him have the treat in your hand.

How to Train 'Down'

1. Have chicken in your hand, make it into a fist.

2. Ask the dog to sit first, if possible, and if the dog responds to that.

3. I like to start from a 'sit' simply because the dog is already half-way there, so it is meant to be easier for him.

4. Still holding the treat to the dog's nose, slowly move your hand towards the floor. Make sure the dog's nose is following your hand the whole time, so that the head, then body will also lower towards the floor to follow the lure. This will then see the dog moving his paws to reposition himself into a down.

5. When the dog lays down, use the cue word 'Down'.

6. Mark by saying 'Good'.

7. Reward the dog with the treat from your hand.

If the dog's bottom goes up, or the dog doesn't lay down, but just stands up, even if the nose is still on the treat- remove your hand with the treat, ask the dog to sit and start again. The dog will eventually figure out that standing up doesn't get him the reward and will try other behaviours, until he gets it and lays down to get the reward. You might have to repeat this a few times.

Leave:

Please, bear in mind that 'leave' is a preventative behaviour! We are teaching the dog NOT to take or touch a certain item. If the dog already has it, then it is too late for a 'leave', that is also why you will train your dog to respond to 'Take' and 'Drop'.

How to Train 'Leave'

1. Have a low-level treat in one hand- like a bit of kibble, or something your dog likes, but not that much.

2. Hand into a fist, at easy reach to the dog. If needed, cover your hand with a bowl or upside-down yogurt pot, so your dog won't hurt your hand. Make sure to hold the pot into place, with the treat under it.

3. The dog will try to get to the treat by scratching, sniffing, licking your hand or the pot. Make sure not to say or do anything while the dog tries to get the treat.

4. When the dog stops trying and backs away, or sits or lays down.

5. Add the cue word 'Leave'.

6. Mark with your chosen word.

7. Reward from your other hand, not on the floor! With the chicken or something your dog absolutely loves.

Progress:

- Add duration, as in how long your dog can keep away from the treat.

- Increase difficulty by opening your hand.
- If the dog tries to get the treat, close your hand again, don't take your hand away.
- Increase the difficulty by using a higher value treat for the dog to leave; or by putting the treat on other surfaces.

Take it & Drop it:

Children seem to love to have all their toys around them, so it is likely that at some point or another, your dog will end up with one of those toys in their mouth. This is when the 'Drop' (or 'Give') comes in handy. By adding the 'Take' behaviour, you can also get the dog to help tidy up! Make sure the kids know how to use 'Drop' or 'Give', so they will understand to stay calm if the dog takes something that belongs to them.

How to Train 'Take'

Items Needed: Treats and one of your dog's toys.

1. Get one of your dog's favourite toys and set it on the ground. Wait for him to pick it up in his mouth. Mark with your chosen word and reward the dog with a treat.

2. Repeat this several times. When he starts picking up the toy without hesitation, start using the cue word 'Take it', then you mark and reward.

3. After a few times of that, test if he will pick it up when you ask.

4. See how many objects he'll pick up! Point to the sock and say, 'Take it'. Mark and reward. Point to a shoe and say take it, etc.

5. If your dog doesn't pick up the toy to start with, make the toy interesting, instead of leaving it on the floor. Play with it, move it around near the dog's mouth to encourage him to pick it up.

How to Train 'Drop'

1. Start with training your dog to take an item in his mouth.

2. Once your dog has the toy, show him a different toy or a treat.

3. When he drops the toy, mark with your chosen word and reward your dog.

4. After a few repetitions, the next time your dog drops the toy and the second you notice his mouth starts opening to release the toy, you'll use the cue word 'Drop', then mark and reward.

5. After practising, practising, and practising, increase the 3Ds!

6. Ask the dog to take a toy and then to drop it. If he does it reliably a few times, he's understood it.

Extra tip: Play tug several times a day. Each time you play the game make sure you use the cue word 'Take it' and when the dog releases the toy, say the cue word 'Drop it'.

You need to keep at it with this exercise, especially because it can be difficult to let go of something precious to your dog. Always keep in mind to not just take the item away from your dog, as he can see it as stealing and will increase his desire to protect it.

Touch:

This is a behaviour I absolutely love, as it is a cue that children and dogs of all ages can use. It can be used not only as a recall, a leave, a prevention from interacting with someone the dog shouldn't approach and more, but we can also then teach the dog to approach our hands and our children's hands with their mouth closed, not teeth on skin at all. It's a perfect win.

How to Train 'Touch'

1. Put a yummy treat in one hand and rub your hands together.

2. Close your hand into a fist, with the treat in it, and put it behind your back.

3. Now, one hand has the treats, the other smells of them.

4. Present the hand that now smells of the treat, to your dog, at the height of his nose (so he doesn't jump to get to it), at a little distance (about 10/20cm), to make it easier at first.

5. When the dog touches the hand with his nose or mouth, mark the behaviour by saying 'Good' and reward him with the yummy treat that you were hiding behind your back. The dog will naturally want to sniff your hand, but the marking must be only for when he touches it!

6. It is important to mark at the right time, exactly when the dog touches your hand with his nose. Not right before or right after, or the dog will

think you've marked and rewarded him for doing something else, NOT for touching your hand!

7. Remember, let the dog come to you! Don't move your hand towards your dog.

8. When your dog has repeated the behaviour successfully a few times, you can add the cue word 'Touch'. Now, when he touches your hand with his nose, say 'Touch', 'Good!' and give him the yummy treat you were hiding behind your back.

9. Repeat a lot! Increase the distance as you go, but don't rush it!

10. Make sure to use the 'Touch' cue when your dog is about to jump on the kids too, as your dog should never practice that behaviour! Your goal is to prevent the jump before it happens using 'Touch'.

Wait:

To my dogs, 'Wait' means 'I'll be back' but it also means 'Don't move until I call you', and of course it always means, 'I am not abandoning you forever, but I'm doing this to keep you safe and polite'. It is a very useful cue! Wait means the dogs won't explode out of the boot of the car when at the park, the dogs won't knock the kids over at the door to get in or out, that the dog won't run into bicycles while off lead, and so on.

How to Train 'Wait'

1. Put a couple of treats or bits of the dog's meal in a bowl.

2. Ask the dog to lie down or to sit- this is not a 'must', but it might help; if this is a problem, the dog can also just be standing.

3. Hold on to the bowl tightly, just in case the dog jumps up and knocks it out of your hand.

4. Start lowering the bowl. If the dog moves towards it or gets up, lift the bowl up again.

5. This process might need to be repeated a few times, until the dog gets that if he gets up or moves, he isn't going to get anything.

6. He will soon learn that if he stays in that position, the bowl will lower, getting the reward closer to him.

7. When the dog can wait long enough for the bowl to reach the floor, use a release word for the dog to have the food almost immediately after the bowl has touched the ground (don't wait and don't tease the dog).

8. Say 'Wait' only when you are confident that your dog can really wait for the bowl to be on the floor.

9. Add duration as you continue training. Never go too fast too soon.

Loose lead walking:

Loose lead walking is up there as one of the most important behaviours to learn! If you have children, you will need to have your dog learning to walk by the pram and, later, the pushchair, but I suggest you start by training the dog to walk nicely on the lead first when it's just you and your dog. Eventually, as you progress the 3Ds, you will then add the pram or pushchair, without your baby in it. Ideally, you will do this before the baby comes, so you feel less stressed by it all. Moreover, if your dog isn't used to it and pulls a lot, he might even pull the pram or pushchair along with your arm, putting the baby at risk. This way, the dog will be trained and ready when your little baby joins the family.

How to Train 'Loose Lead Walking,'

Make sure your dog wears a comfortable harness. It should be a 'Y' shaped front and should not be too big or too small. You should be able to place two fingers between the body of the dog and any part of the harness that touches their body. If you can fit more or less than two fingers, the size needs to be adjusted.

The lead should feel comfortable in your hand, not slippery, not too bulky, not too hard, or too thin. When working with children, I encourage you to look for a lead like a Stormridge lead that has an extra handle in the middle, so the adult can hold the main handle, while the child holds the end of the lead. That way, if the dog were to pull or stop suddenly, or need support during an outing, the adult would be the one to feel the pull or variation of the lead and dog's movement. While the child would be none the wiser. Also, this means that the child would not suddenly get pulled, risk falling over, or getting hurt.

Tips
- Start training in a location that doesn't trigger the dog, so somewhere calm, with no

distractions and where the dog is comfortable and calm.

- Ideally, you can start training in the house or your garden.
- For 'Loose Lead Walking' there are a lot of techniques that can be used, but as a very basic thing to remember, regardless of which technique you use and whether you have the pram with you or not, if the dog pulls, you stop walking! If you carry one walking, you are basically telling the dog that it's ok to pull. By stopping, the dog won't be able to go anywhere the pulling will not be reinforced.

This is one of my favourite methods to use with and without the pram.

1. Have lots of high value treats (chicken, hotdogs, cheddar cheese, etc.). Bring a variety of treats, to keep the dog more interested and able to cope with distractions.

2. Take one step, mark with the chosen word and reward with a treat.

3. Take another step, mark and reward; and so on.

4. If the dog tries to jump up, place the reward on the floor, instead of rewarding hand to mouth.

5. When the walk comes naturally and the dog is always by your side, you can add a cue word. Some people say 'Heel', but I love saying 'With Me', I think it gives us a sense that we are connected, and I like that.

6. Now you should be able to take one step, say 'With Me', mark and reward; one step, 'With Me', mark and reward, and so on.

7. Don't rush things, so before adding more steps, make sure your dog understands that 'With Me' means, 'we walk together'.

8. We'll do that by rewarding the dog as we walk, not as we stand still, so while you are taking that one step (not before and not after) and your dog is with you (not left behind, nor ahead of you), you'll say 'With Me', mark and reward.

9. Practice, practice, practice!

10. When you are satisfied with that and feel confident your dog knows that 'With Me' means walking together, you are ready to progress by adding one more step.

11. Now you're at two steps, 'With Me', mark and reward; three steps, 'With Me', mark and reward, and so on

12. When you are happy with that, add another step!

13. Count three steps, 'with me', mark and reward; four steps, 'with me', mark and reward, and so on.

Carry on adding steps, but only when the dog is ready and there's no more pulling of the lead.

Don't rush into anything. Going slower will add bonding, value, and reinforcement to walking nicely on the lead- with you!

The environment is super important while training your dog to walk nicely on the lead. If your dog walks brilliantly in the house, but still a little distracted in the garden, then he isn't ready for the outside world yet. If he's great in the house, fantastic in the garden, then take him out the front door, but don't head over to the doggy park just yet, that would be too big of a leap to take. Build it up gradually.

Recall:

Having your dog off the lead while you are out with the kids, whether as babies or older, is so much better! Not only is your dog free to make his own choices, but you will also have a bit of freedom. Yes, you still need to have your eyes everywhere to make sure your dog isn't getting in any trouble and the kids are still alive. But it is so much nicer to do without your hands holding the lead. Moreover, I think that a great recall is essential. You need to be able to call your dog back when it's time to go because the kids are tired, or injured, or need the toilet, or a snack, or they forgot their second favourite toy, or the sky is too blue…

Once again, involve the kids in training recall! For this one, games like 'Hide and Seek' are great, but I also love the **'Touch'**, which you would have already worked on.

Peekaboo:

'Peekaboo', also known as 'Middle', like 'Touch'- is great recall behaviour, good fun to teach and do. The older kids can also train the dog to respond to it. This cue also improves and builds the bonding between humans and dogs- it gives dogs a sense of security that us humans will look after them. Not to mention that it's great when you are walking with a pushchair in a narrow bit of a walkway or sidewalk and can use 'Peakaboo' when someone walks by.

And it works brilliantly when holding the baby in a sling too.

How to Train 'Peekaboo'

1. Have two treats, one in each hand.

2. Stand in front of the dog and keep your legs hip width apart.

3. Lure the dog to walk behind you and continue to follow your hand that has a treat in it.

4. Give him that first treat when he's behind you. You can feed your hand to his mouth, or, even better, place the reward on the floor just behind you, or even between your legs. Just make sure the treat isn't far from your dog.

5. With the other hand, lure the dog to walk between your legs.

6. When you see the head of your dog poking out between your legs, the body of the dog should be slightly touching your legs, mark with your chosen word and reward your dog.

7. Once you are confident, the dog understands the behaviour, and he is repeating it nicely, you can add the cue work 'Peekaboo' when the dog is in the middle of your legs.

8. Keep repeating the exercise until you are happy and sure that your dog understands what 'Peekaboo' means.

9. Once you are 100% sure the dog knows what to do, you can stop giving the first treat, and just reward him for completing the exercise.

<u>Settle in a safe space</u> (the dog nook):

I might have kept this one last, but it is an essential part of preparing your dog for the arrival of a small human in the house. So, if you are trying to select what to train your dog to do, this cue has to be done!

Use a mat or doggy bed your dog likes and always knows, so his scent will be on it. Place that mat or bed in a playpen or behind a gate, in the room the dog will be in- the dog nook. It would be good for the dog to be in a quiet space, but not somewhere where nobody ever goes to. Your dog would still want to be able to see you and be part of your life, but also have a safe place to go to.

Remember, to help him love the dog nook, you need to know what your dog loves!

Does he love hotdogs? Fab, go chop some up (nice and small, think pea-size)!

Does he love his old smelly teddy? Great, go get it!

For the purpose of this cue, I will use hotdogs as a reward, but you can use anything that your dog finds super highly rewarding – i.e. cheese, an old sock, etc.

Start by tossing a piece of hotdog in the dog bed. Make sure your dog knows you had that food and that he's seen you toss it in there. As he builds up the confidence of stepping into the bed, make sure you don't shut the gate or door right way, as that would make him feel trapped... when he's in, have treats falling from the sky, so to speak, as if it was raining hotdogs!

If the dog leaves the bed or given space, the treats must stop! The fun only happens in there!

Use Mealtimes to Train!

Every meal should be served in that space... however, add a little twist! Make sure your dog knows that it's mealtime, he's watched you prepare it, and put it in a bowl (slow feeder/maize bowls are much better!), then watch as your dog follows you to the designated space- their dog nook. There you'll put the bowl inside the dog nook and close the gate, keeping your dog outside the dog nook with you! He'll want his food, so he will want to go inside the room! When he asks to go inside, open the gate or door, and allow him to go in and have his meal.

While he's eating you can close the gate or door, but don't go away, stay there and wait for him to finish eating. Once he's finished, open the door. Don't wait for him to ask you to open it, the second he's done with the food, open the gate casually for him... don't ask him to come out. Don't say anything... wait for him to decide for himself. If you aren't sure whether he's finished or not, as you might have a door between you and the dog, estimate how long it normally takes him to finish a meal and open the door within that time.

What we don't want to happen is for your dog to have finished eating and then ask to be let out. If he asks to be let out it feels more like he doesn't want to be in there, but we want to focus our attention on teaching him that he does, that's why we want him to ask to be let in for his meals.

Work that nose!

Nose work, also called scent work, is a great way for your dog to channel his energy into something positive and fun. It keeps him busy and gets him tired in a positive and mentally stimulating way. There are many ways to do some scent work! For example, a great way is by using puzzle solving toys, such as the ones you can get from the pet shops (i.e. doggy puzzles; ruffle rugs, West Paws, Kongs, etc.).

Say that you are using a West Paws toy, stuff it with yummy things (one of my dogs' favourite treats is natural yoghurt, with blueberries and bits of ham... I normally put it in the freezer for a bit, so that the yoghurt is hard and it's more difficult for the dog to lick, which means he'll be at it for longer... and the crate won't be covered in yoghurt!).

I have the dog with me, by the gate or door and let him smell the West Paws toy. I really want him to want it! I will then put the West Paws toy in the crate and have the dog follow it. Because that toy is challenging, fun and rewarding, he will have a sense of achievement while using it... all this, while being in the dog nook! As he licks the West Paws toy, casually close the door... and only reopen it when you see he's done with the toy. Just like with his meal, make sure not to wait until he asks to come out. Open the gate or door when you see he's starting to leave the West Paws toy, which also means he's almost done with it, or getting tired of the hard work it can be.

If you don't have a West Paws toy ready, then use a snuffle mat or rug, or other form of enrichment items! Have a few treats hidden in the item of your choice, let your dog smell it, then place it inside the dog nook and have him follow. Once inside, close the gate and watch him have fun, develop his nose senses and get tired doing it! When you start noticing that he might have found all the treats, or he starts leaving the area with his toy, and looking around more, open the gate again. He's probably about to be done and you don't want him to ask to be let out. Don't make a fuss when letting him out, simply open the door and let him do his thing. Make sure to take the puzzle toy out of the dog nook and put it away until the next time.

If you notice your doggy getting tired and sleepy while finishing with his puzzles, let him sleep in there... what a better way of falling in love with it?

Alone Time

Normally, dog nook training can take two or three weeks. Every dog is different, and some get used to it faster than others. However, as a guideline, you should expect around 3 weeks' training. That also means, you can't suddenly leave your dog alone in the dog nook for hours. You need to build the time slowly. At first, leave him alone for 2 minutes, then 5 minutes, then 10, etc.

Always consider the needs of your dog! Make sure he's gone to the toilet before he's left in the dog nook. And remember, 2 little minutes for you could be an eternity for your dog. Be kind and don't rush it.

Extra tips:

If you notice your dog being sleepy, pick him up and put him in his dog nook. If your dog's too big to be picked up, get him, using a very relaxed tone (whispering, perhaps), to follow you and you accompany him to the bed. Stay there until he falls asleep. If he wakes up or can't settle, don't worry, let him come out (don't close the gate), better luck next time.

Don't leave a bowl of water too close to your dog's bed when they're sleeping, especially over nighttime or if you need to go out for a couple of hours. If your dog accidentally knocks it over, his bed and the rest of the space will be wet, making it uncomfortable for most dogs.

Never leave your dog wearing a collar unattended, especially behind a gate. The collar could get attached and stuck to one of the bars, injuring – or worse – your dog.

Music can help! Some studies show that Reggae and Soft Rock music is the best to leave your dog alone with. *

Pet Remedy offers a range of good products that can help calm your dog down when stressed.

* 'The effect of different genres of music on the stress levels of kennelled dogs', Scottish SPCA, 2017

It Started With A Sit

Chapter 16:

Basic Canine Body Language

I am a strong believer in learning to speak the language of dogs, because if we were to understand how dogs communicate, we can and will prevent dog-related injuries and even fatalities from happening.

If we understand the signs of a dog getting upset, we can stop that interaction. Such as calling the dog away from the situation, giving him a place or easy game to rest and make him feel better and happier again.

Here are some basic canine body language signals to get you started and that you can also show your little humans as they grow:

When the dog says **'No, thank you.'**, some features to pay attention to are:

- Mouth closed

- Ears pinned back

- Tail between the legs

- Cowering away/lowering the body to the ground.

When the dog says **'Yes, please.'** some features to notice are:

- Mouth open, tongue hanging out

- Ears are in the normal position for the breed (for example, up and pointy for German Shepherds, floppy by the side for Beagles)

- Soft eyes (the white of the eyes is not visible)

© KIDS AROUND DOGS

It Started With A Sit

In Summary

Every step I took and everything I did in life, was taken and done for a reason.

Leaving Switzerland, meeting Gary in London, getting married, adopting Pixel, having a Molly, losing our beautiful boy, and adopting Wilco... these were all steps I was meant to take, which led me where I am today. Now, I am a dog behaviourist, a dog trainer, the founder of Kids Around Dogs®, a mother and wife. I have helped thousands of dogs and hundreds of children to live a better life together, whether under the same roof or simply by sharing the same planet.

I have made mistakes, but hopefully learned from them too. I have learned from dogs and children more than I have ever imagined possible and I am still learning from them every day. My child and my dogs have taught me about love and heartbreak and remind me every day that life is challenging, but that it can also be made easier with a bit of fun and playfulness.

The pages you have just finished reading were my first years with dogs and into parenthood, but more, oh so much more is to come! I can't wait for you to continue my journey with me!

Acknowledgements

I could probably write another book just to thank everyone who has contributed to my story in some way, but I will try to keep it brief, or as brief as I can.

Thank you to my wonderful editor, who is also an amazing dog and cat behaviourist, and KAD Approved Professional, Ruby Lesley and her assistants Marmalade and Spark.

To my mamma, papà and my brother Davide, *grazie* for everything you do, even from miles away.

I am grateful to have married into a lovely, understanding and scrabble obsessed family, John, Christine, Charlotte, Mark, Marianne, Alex, Oliver, Katie, and Junior & Tara (the cats).

Friendship is extremely important to me, and I am so lucky to have Grainne, Lynn, Carrie, and Nikki in my life.

To Grainne goes a special thank you. You are the most amazing friend anyone could have, and I thank my lucky stars every day for the gift of your friendship.

Thank you, Max! I am so happy I get to see you growing to be such a wonderful young man.

This book would certainly not be here without the love, help and support of my husband Gary, who has also designed the cover!

Thank you, Molly, my wonderful, funny, clever, and cheeky girl. I love you <3

Thank you, Wilco, for giving me the strength I needed and for finding your way to us.

An extremely furry thank you to my girl Winnie, for helping me and so many children out there to overcome their fear of dogs and for simply being you!

I am thankful to Mario, for opening the world of cats up to me and for his silly obsession with Pokémon cards!

To my boy Pixel, thank you for watching over us and for making me a mother.

Thank you to all the dogs I had the privilege of working with over the years, and the many kids I had the honour of educating: you guys are the real teachers!

To all the KAD Kids Around Dogs® Approved Professionals, who are everywhere in the world, helping children to understand, respect and love dogs and to allow kids and dogs to have a happy life together; thank you guys. From the bottom of my heart, thank you for being part of the KAD family!

It Started With A Sit

Recommended Links

Kids Around Dogs®
www.kidsarounddogs.co.uk

Pocodogs
www.pocodogs.co.uk

Family Paws
www.familypaws.com

Animal Assisted Intervention International
www.aai-int.org

Animal Centre Education:
www.tilleyfarm.org.uk

Welfare for Animals
www.welfare4animals.org

BeKind Rescue (KAD Approved Rescue)
www.bekindrescue.com

Sprocker Assist (KAD Approved Rescue)
www.sprockerassist.org

Dog Welfare Alliance
www.thedogwelfarealliance.co.uk

Pet Remedy
www.petremedy.co.uk

Stormridge Pet (dog leads)
stormridgepet@gmail.com

My Anxious Dog (Dogs in Yellow)
www.myanxiousdog.co.uk

NHS
www.nhs.uk/pregnancy

213

About the Author

Debby Lucken is a fully qualified dog behaviourist with the International School of Canine Psychology and a force-free dog trainer with the Institute of Modern Dog Trainers.

She is a member of the Pet Professional Network, ICAN International Companion Animal Network, INTODogs, the Pet Professional Guild, the Society for Companion Animal Studies (SCAS), the Dog Welfare Alliance and the Pet Professional Network.

Debby has almost a decade of experience working with dogs, and she particularly enjoys assisting kids to teach and raise their dogs to be great family companions. Many of her clients are also great emotional assistance dogs in schools and nursing homes.

Debby is the founder of Kids Around Dogs® (KAD), which is an association of qualified professionals who specialise in working with families and schools to help children and dogs live in harmony together.

Moreover, Debby has designed a successful protocol to overcome the fear of dogs in kids and adults, which all KAD Approved Professionals are qualified to use.

Debby's work with KAD has been awarded the SBS Theo Paphitis Award in May 2022.

Debby is based in Poole, Dorset, with her husband Gary, their daughter Molly, their 2 doggies Wilco the Pug and Winnie the Golden Retriever, and Mario the cat.

Dorset is where Debby runs her dog training and behavioural business under the name of Pocodogs. She delivers lessons and webinars globally (she is also bilingual, speaking English and Italian, which allows her to help more professionals and dog handlers around the world).

Kids Around Dogs® is on Facebook, Instagram, YouTube, TikTok and X

www.kidsarounddogs.co.uk

It Started With A Sit

It Started With A Sit